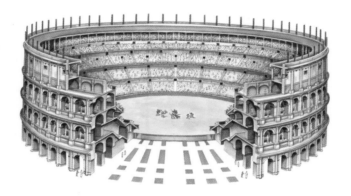

THE ARCHITECTURE OF
ANCIENT ROME

THE ARCHITECTURE OF
ANCIENT ROME

An illustrated guide to the glorious classical
heritage of the Roman Empire

NIGEL RODGERS • CONSULTANT: DR. HAZEL DODGE FSA

LORENZ BOOKS

This edition is published by Lorenz Books,
an imprint of Anness Publishing Ltd,
Blaby Road, Wigston, Leicestershire LE18 4SE
info@anness.com

www.lorenzbooks.com; www.annesspublishing.com

Anness Publishing has a new picture agency outlet for
publishing, promotions or advertising. Please visit our website
www.practicalpictures.com for more information.

Publisher: Joanna Lorenz
Editorial Director: Helen Sudell
Editors: Joy Wotton and Elizabeth Woodland
Designer: Nigel Partridge
Cover Designer: Balley Design Associates
Illustrations and maps: Vanessa Card, Peter Bull Art Studio
Production Controller: Wendy Lawson

© Anness Publishing Ltd 2013

A CIP catalogue record for this book is available from the British Library.

PUBLISHER'S NOTE
Although the advice and information in this book are believed to be accurate and true at the time of going to
press, neither the authors nor the publisher can accept any legal responsibility or liability for any errors or
omissions that may have been made.

Front cover, clockwise from left to right: Baths of Antonius Pius at Carthage; The Pantheon, Rome; The Forum Romanum, Rome;
The Colosseum, Rome.
Front cover flap: A cutaway section of the Colosseum.
Back cover flap: Hadrian's Wall.
Back cover, clockwise from left to right: The Forum Romanum, Rome; bakery in Pompeii; Pompeii's Forum; Italian vineyards;
The Colosseum, Rome; map of Pompeii.
Page 1: A cutaway section of the Colosseum.
Page 2: The scene wall of the theatre at Sabratha.
Page 3: Sabratha, Antonine Temple.
Page 4: House of the Dancing Faun, Pompeii.
Page 5: Part of Nero's Domus Aurea in central Rome.

ACKNOWLEDGEMENTS
Alan Hakim: 2, 3. Ancient Art and Architecture Collection: 100b, 101b, 125b. Art Archive: Dagli Orti 40–1, /Dagli Orti: 8b,
20tl, 22t, 35b, 38b, 47b, 49b, 68l and r, 69t, 70t, 90b, 94t, 96t and b, 97b, 108b, 109t, 115b, 119b, 120t, 122t and b, 123t, /Bardo
Mus. Tunis/Dagli Orti 111t, /Archaeological Mus. Madrid/ Dagli Orti/ Dagli Orti 11m, /Bibliothèque des Arts Décoratifs Paris/Dagli Orti 126–7,
/Album J. Enrique Molina 14–15, 47t, /Historical Picture Archive 17t, /Harper Collins Publishers 20b, /Museo della Civita Romana
Rome/Dagli Orti 52b, 54t, /Museo Capitolino Rome/Dagli Orti 53b, /Private Collection/ Eileen Tweedy 62, /Archaeological
Mus. Naples/Dagli Orti 85b, 106b, 107t, /Nicolas Sapieha 89t, /Archaeological Museum Istanbul/Dagli Orti 98t, /Diozesan-
museum Trier/Dagli Orti 117, /Ephesus Mus. Turkey/Dagli Orti 118t. Bridgeman Art Library: 20tr, 23b, 27t, 51b, 74t, 112t,
128–9. Corbis: 11m, 45t, 63b, /Araldo de Luca 66b, 69b, 77b, 86b, 109b, /Mimmo Jodice 8t, 74b, 75t, 84b, 85t, 88t, 89b, 94b,
95b, 104t, 106t, /Lawrence Manning 9b, /Michael S. Yamashita 28t, 53t, /Sandro Vannini 10m, 10r, 110b, /Roger Ressmeyer 12m,
102–3, 104t, /Andrea Jemolo 16b, 44b, /Paul Almasy 18b, 123b, /Alinari Archives 19t, 27b, 51t, /Gustavo Tomisch 19b, /Carmen
Redondo 21b, 24t, 80b, 81t, /ML Sinibaldi 22b, /Angelo Hornak 23t, 34b, /Peter M Wilson 24b, /Bill Ross 25t, /Vittoriano
Rastelli 25br, /Dennis Marsico 26b, /Archivo Iconografico, S.A. 29b, 64b, 71t, 114b, /David Lees 29t, /Michael Nicholson 30–1,
115t, 120b, /Vince Streano 32b, /Hans Georg Roth 33t, /Richard T. Nowitz 34t, /John Heseltine 39b, 63t, /Ludovic Maisant
50t, /Roger Wood 52t, 57b, 84t, 93tl, 110t, 112b, 113b, /Yann Arthus-Bertrand 56t, /Vanni Archive 57t, 61t, 65b, 87b, 99b,
105b, 109t, /Tony Brown/Eye Ubiquitous 58t, /Ruggero Vanni 58b, 66t, 116t, /Freelance Consulting Service 59t, /Bettmann
60b, 98b, /Mark L. Stephenson 61b, /Paul Hardy 71b, /Massimo Listri 76b, /Werner Forman 86t, /Macduff Everton 91t, 92, 93b,
/David Ball 95t, /Stapleton Collection 99t, /Nik Wheeler 100t, /Stephanie Colasanti 114t, /Richard Klune 116b, /Hanan Isachar
119t, /Wolfgang Kaehler 121, /Reuters 124t, /Kevin Schafer 124b, /Benjamin Rondel 125t. Photo Scala, Florence: /© 1990 16tl,
17b, 37, 49t, 54b, 59b, 64t, 67t, 70b, 93tr, 111b, /© 1999 13l, 28b, /© 1990 Fondo Edifici di Culto – Min. dell'Interno 48t,
/© 1990/courtesy of the Ministero Beni e Att. Culturali 2–3, 11l, 18t, 21t, 42b, 46b, 60t, 72–3, 76t, 78t and b, 79t and b, 80t,
90t, 91b, /© 2003/Fotografica Foglia 82–3, /© 2003 Luciano Romano 88b, /© 2003/HIP 101t. Karita Lightfoot: 4.

CONTENTS

INTRODUCTION

Rome was the first cosmopolis. By AD100 it had a population of over one million, unmatched by any other city. Greek was spoken almost as commonly in its streets as Latin, for educated Romans were bilingual. The resulting Graeco-Roman cultural fusion was most marked in architecture. Greek classical architecture relied on columns and porticoes of stone and marble. The Romans, lacking such good stone, exploited concrete to create vaults, arches and domes. The Pantheon (built *c.* AD124–8) unites a sublime Greek portico with a brilliantly designed concrete Roman dome. The Romans, who never believed that form had to follow function, used classical columns less to support roofs or porticoes than for decorative purposes, humanizing massive, sometimes blank structures. Their columns employed a distinct classical language based ultimately on the human form.

Despite Rome's own vastness, humanity remained the measure and ideal of Roman classical culture. This classical style proved so flexible and inspirational that it influenced Byzantine, Romanesque (Norman), Renaissance, Baroque, Neoclassical and other styles well into the 20th century. Most great Western cities reveal this Roman influence, as the Capitol in Washington, St Paul's Cathedral in London and the Arc de Triomphe in Paris attest. The Romans built lavishly across their empire, founding or refounding cities. Some, since abandoned – Lepcis Magna in Libya, Palmyra in Syria, Pompeii in Italy – now vividly display the wonders of Roman architecture and city life, as does the city of Rome itself.

Left: Arches of the Colosseum in Rome, dedicated in AD80 by the emperor Titus.

ROME'S ENDURING LEGACY

Above: This fresco of the Three Graces from the House of Titus Dentatus Panthera in Pompeii of c. AD79 epitomizes the brilliance of Roman art near the empire's zenith.

Below: The Forum Romanum, the ancient heart of the imperial city, was adorned over many centuries with temples and monuments.

The Roman world lies all around us. Even this book is written in the Roman (or Latin) alphabet. Although the Roman empire in the West collapsed more than 1,500 years ago, Rome's fascination and relevance to the modern world are today as strong as ever.

THE CULTURAL DEBT

Western culture is manifestly indebted to Rome and so too is that of Eastern Europe, through the Byzantine civilization which Russia perpetuated and, more indirectly, the Islamic world, conqueror of much of the former Roman world.

Although knowledge of Latin may no longer be common – few people now spice their speeches with Latin quotes – it remains very useful in the legal, medical and scientific worlds. Almost half the words in the English language derive from Latin, while Spanish, French and Italian are all Romance languages, the direct descendants of Latin. Similarly, the legal systems of most Romance-speaking countries, whether in continental Europe or Latin America, remain based on the majestic and logical edifice of Roman law. Symbolically, this was only finally summarized in the 6th century AD in Constantinople (Istanbul), the East Roman capital, after the fall of the Western empire. Rome's world survived the fall of its power.

In a more concrete sense, many of Europe's great cities – London, Paris, Lyons, Cologne, Milan, Seville, Vienna – were originally Roman, for Romans had a genius for choosing the right spot for cities that would thrive, endure and revive even after barbarians sacked them. Similarly, Europe's roads often follow or parallel routes pioneered by Roman road-builders. Roman brilliance as engineers, soldiers and as lawyers has never been disputed, but their literary and architectural achievements have some-times been overlooked by those obsessed with Greece. Rome was never merely the channel through which Greek culture reached Western and Northern Europe: it provided its own unique input.

Observers looking at the Colosseum in Rome, the aqueduct of the Pont du Gard in France, the ruins of Ephesus in Turkey or of Lepcis Magna in Libya, may be awed by the splendour of Roman cities but they are seeing only the ruins of ruins. Rome's huge edifices were plundered by succeeding generations who saw in them only convenient quarries for marble, stone and brick. This applies even to the Colosseum. Revered as early as *c.* AD700 when Bede wrote of it as the epitome of *Christian* Rome's grandeur, its destruction continued until Pope Benedict XIV declared it a site sacred to Christian martyrs in 1749, so preserving what remained.

Our knowledge of the ancient world, while growing steadily as new archaeological findings supplement older literary sources, remains tantalizingly incomplete.

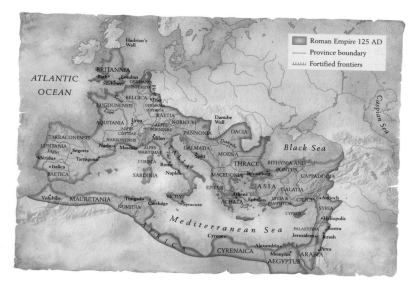

Left: Rome's empire, while centred on the Mediterranean, spread Graeco-Roman civilization far to the north, west and south, founding cities and extending its language, religion and laws in a way that has proved almost indestructible.

For half a millennium the Roman world united the lands of the Mediterranean basin (for the only time in their history) and pushed deep into northern Europe. It was in some ways very different from today's world, with different ideas about gods and the afterlife, the existence of slavery and social hierarchy, and yet it was a world whose inhabitants had many of the same aspirations, anxieties and dislikes as our own. Many aspects of everyday Roman life have been preserved at Pompeii, that urban time capsule buried by a volcano just as the empire neared its zenith. Its stunning wall paintings indicate just how much has been lost.

THE FIRST WORLD CITY

Rome still fascinates as the first cosmopolis, the first truly global city. As its population surged past the one million mark, it drew in philosophers, merchants, slaves and adventurers from across the ancient world, from the borders of Scotland in the north to Iraq in the east. The first to offer the excitement and challenges of a world city, it also pioneered ways of supplying, entertaining and controlling such unprecedented numbers.

Every age, looking back afresh, can find aspects of Roman architecture to admire and emulate, or to abhor and avoid. Some disapprovingly see obese senators, debauched emperors, Christian virgins eaten by lions, gladiators slaughtering each other and slaves toiling beneath the lash. Others glimpse white-colonnaded cities with libraries, theatres and baths, arrow-straight roads spreading prosperity from Britain to the Middle East, broad-minded governors ensuring religious tolerance and many centuries of political stability.

Napoleon Bonaparte modelled his short-lived militaristic empire on Rome's, emulating its eagles, triumphal arches and careers for all, irrespective of national or social backgrounds. In the 20th century, more vicious dictators notoriously copied his worst features. In the 18th century, many liberal Europeans saw in the balanced British political system some of the virtues of *Republican* Rome, which later inspired moderates and extremists in the French Revolution. Today, the genius of Rome lives on and is revealed to us through our laws, language, art, religions and the extraordinary architecture.

Above: The Library of Celsus in Ephesus, Asia Minor, testifies to that province's exuberant prosperity in the 2nd century AD.

TIMELINE

Above: Julius Caesar

As this timeline of political and cultural events reveals, ancient Rome had a remarkably rich political and cultural history. As Rome's power grew across the Mediterranean, she adopted and adapted other cultures, notably Greece's, disseminating north and west the resulting culture, usually called Graeco-Roman. But Rome was never a mere conduit for Hellenic civilization. This is especially true in architecture and literature. In the late Republic (150–30BC), Greek culture seemed set to overwhelm that of Rome, but already Roman architects were making wholly original use of vaults and arches. Similarly Latin literature evolved its own distinctive voice. There is no exact equivalent in Greek literature of Virgil, ancient Rome's epic poet, nor of Petronius, the racy satirist. Roman women had far more freedom than Greek, if mainly within marriage, and many slaves were freed.

All dates given before 350BC are approximate. The Romans dated all events *ab urbe condita*, from the legendary foundation by Romulus of their city in 753BC. Only in the 5th century AD did the present Christian calendar supersede the old Roman calendar system.

POLITICAL EVENTS: 753–101BC

753BC Legendary founding of the city of Rome by Romulus.
c. **650–510** Etruscans dominant in Rome.
509 Expulsion of the last king, Tarquinius Superbus; foundation of the Republic.
496 Rome defeats Latins at the Battle of Lake Regilius.
451 Twelve Tables of the Law published.
405–396 Siege and capture of Veii.
390 Sack of Rome by Gauls.
338 Defeat of the Latin League: Roman power extends into Campania.
312 Censorship of Appius Claudius.
298–290 Third Samnite War.
275 Romans defeat Pyrrhus and conquer southern Italy.
264–241 First Punic War.
241 Sicily becomes first Roman province.
218–202 Second Punic War.
216 Roman army crushed at battle of Cannae by Hannibal.
202 Scipio defeats Hannibal at Zama.
200–196 Second Macedonian War.
190 Seleucid King Antiochus III defeated at Magnesia: Rome arbiter of the east.
167 Sack of Epirus: 150,000 Greeks enslaved.
146 Sack of cities of Carthage and Corinth: Greece, Macedonia and Africa become Roman provinces.
135–132 First Sicilian Slave War.
133BC Tiberius Gracchus, tribune, killed; kingdom of Pergamum left to Rome.

Above: The ruins of Carthage, once Rome's greatest enemy, then a thriving Roman city.

CULTURAL EVENTS: 753–101BC

c. **620BC** Draining of Roman Forum.
c. **540** *Ambush of Troilus by Achilles* wall painting from Tomb of the Bulls, Tarquinia; traditional date of building of first Curia (Senate House).
510 Building of first Capitoline Temple.
500 Capitoline Wolf bronze; Apollo of Veii.
483 Building of Temple of Castor et Pollux.
c. **390** Wounded Chimaera bronze.
378 Building of Servian Wall.
312 Building of first Roman road, Via Appia, and first aqueduct, Aqua Appia.
300 Bronze bust of "Brutus the Liberator".
275 Eratosthenes in Alexandria works out earth's circumference.
264 First gladiatorial contest in Rome.
254 Birth of Plautus.
239 Birth of poet Ennius at Rudiae.
234 Birth of Cato the Censor.
220 Circus Flaminius built in Rome.
212 Archimedes killed at Syracuse.
204 *Miles Gloriosus* by Plautus staged.
195 Birth of Terence in Africa.
186 Senate issues edict against Bacchic rites.
179 Basilica Aemilia and Pons Aemilius built.
170 Basilica Sempronia built.
169 Death of Ennius.
166–159 Terence's major plays produced.
c. **150** "First Pompeian Style" of wall painting emerges.
144 Construction of Aqua Marcia.
106BC Birth of Cicero.

Above: Painting from the Tomb of the Bulls c. 550BC, a fine example of Etruscan art.

Above: Augustus

Above: Tiberius

Above: Caligula

Above: Claudius

Above: Nero

POLITICAL EVENTS: 100BC–1BC

107–100BC Marius consul six times; reforms army; defeats Cimbri and Teutones.
88 Sulla marches on Rome.
82–80 Sulla dictator in Rome.
73–71 Slave revolt of Spartacus crushed by Crassus and Pompey.
66 Pompey given huge command in east.
63 Consulship of Cicero, Pompey captures Jerusalem.
60 First Triumvirate: Caesar, Pompey, Crassus.
59 Caesar consul for first time.
58–51 Caesar's conquest of Gaul. Death of Crassus at Battle of Carrhae. Start of Civil War.
48 Pompey defeated at Pharsalus: Caesar meets Cleopatra.
44 Caesar becomes perpetual dictator; subsequently assassinated.
42 Republicans defeated at Philippi: empire divided, Octavian taking the west, Mark Antony the east.
40–38 Parthians invade Syria.
36 Antony launches major offensive against the Parthians.
31 Battle of Actium: Octavian defeats Antony and Cleopatra.
30 Cleopatra and Antony commit suicide; annexation of Egypt, reunification of empire.
27 "The Republic restored"; Octavian assumes title Augustus.
18 Lex Julia: law against adultery.
16–9 Alpine and Balkan areas annexed.
12 Death of Agrippa.

Above: Detail of the Ara Pacis (Altar of Peace), dedicated under Augustus in 9BC.

CULTURAL EVENTS: 100BC–1BC

100BC Temple of Neptune in Rome.
96 Birth of Lucretius.
84 Birth of Catullus.
82–79 Building of *Tabularium* (Records Office).
c. **80** Second Pompeian Style of painting develops.
70 Birth of Virgil.
65 Birth of Horace.
60 Cicero published his *Catiline Orations*.
c. **55** Building of Theatre of Pompey.
50s Catullus writing greatest poems.
c. **54** Birth of Propertius.
46 Forum of Caesar and Basilica Julia begun.
44–21 Strabo the geographer active.
c. **45** Cicero *Scipio's Dream*.
43 Birth of Ovid; murder of Cicero.
37 Temple of Mars Ultor in Augustus' Forum, Rome, begun (finished 2BC).
29 Virgil's *Georgics*.
23 Horace's *Odes* books 1–3.
21 Agrippa marries Julia.
20 Prima Porta statue of Augustus.
19 Death of Virgil and Tibullus; publication of *The Aeneid*; building of the Aqua Julia; Start of Maison Carrée and Pont du Gard at Nimes.
13 Building of Theatre of Marcellus.
9 First edition of Ovid's *Ars Amatoria*; Ara Pacis dedicated.
4 Birth of philosopher and playwright Seneca near Cordova.

Above: The Arch of Septimius Severus in the Forum Romanum, Rome.

Above: Domitian

Above: Trajan

Above: Hadrian

Above: Marcus Aurelius

Above: Septimius Severus

POLITICAL EVENTS: AD1–199

AD6 Judaea becomes Roman province.
9 Loss of three legions under Varrus in Germany; withdrawal to Rhine frontier.
14 Augustus dies; Tiberius becomes emperor.
30/33 Crucifixion of Jesus.
37 Death of Tiberius; accession of Caligula.
41 Caligula assassinated: accession of Claudius.
43 Invasion of Britain.
54 Death of Claudius; accession of Nero, Seneca and Burrus chief ministers.
62 Burrus dies and end of Seneca's influence; Nero becomes increasingly extravagant.
64 Great Fire of Rome: Nero makes Christians scapegoats and begins rebuilding Rome.
68–9 Suicide of Nero: Year of the Four Emperors.
70 Capture and sack of Jerusalem by Titus.
79 Pompeii and Herculaneum destroyed.
81 Death of Titus; accession of Domitian.
96 Assassination of Domitian; Nerva succeeds.
98 Death of Nerva; accession of Trajan.
101–6 Dacian wars.
113–17 Parthian campaign ends in defeat.
117 Death of Trajan; accession of Hadrian.
121–2 Hadrian visits Britain.
138 Death of Hadrian.
161 Marcus Aurelius, Lucius Verus co-emperors.
165–6 Plague brought back from Parthia by legionaries.
167 Marcomanni and Quadi attack Italy.
180 Death of Marcus on the Danube; accession of Commodus.
192 Assassination of Commodus; civil war.
193 Septimius Severus emperor in Rome.

Above: Human body caught in the eruption of Vesuvius that destroyed Pompeii in AD79.

CULTURAL EVENTS AD1–199

AD2 Forum of Augustus dedicated.
8 Banishment of Ovid to Black Sea.
18 Death of Ovid.
27 Building of Tiberius' villa at Capri.
c. 40–3 Birth of Martial; Claudius builds new harbour near Ostia and Aqua Claudia.
60 Birth of Juvenal; *De re rustica* by Columella.
64–8 Nero builds the *Domus Aurea*.
65 Deaths of Seneca and Lucan.
66 Suicide of Petronius, author of *Satyricon*.
79 Death of Pliny the Elder.
80 Colosseum dedicated.
82 Arch of Titus; start of construction of Palatine Palace; first of Martial's *Epigrams*.
100 Pliny the Younger's *Panegyrics* on Trajan.
100–10 Tacitus: *Histories and Annals*.
103 Trajan's new inner harbour near Ostia.
110 First of Juvenal's *Satires*.
115 Arch of Trajan at Benevento.
112–14 Dedication of Forum and Column of Trajan; death of Pliny the Younger in Bithynia.
115 Library of Celsus in Ephesus.
120–30s Hadrian builds the Pantheon, Hadrian's Wall, Basilica at London, Villa at Tivoli.
c. 127 Apuleius born in Africa.
131 Hadrian establishes Panhellenion and completes Temple of Zeus in Athens.
140–50s Ptolemy active in Alexandria.
150–60s Galen active as doctor in Rome; Apuleius' *The Golden Ass*.
174–80 *Meditations* of Marcus Aurelius, composed during wars on Danube.
193 Column of Marcus Aurelius completed.

Above: Arches of the Colosseum in Rome, dedicated in AD80 by the emperor Titus.

Above: Elagabalus

Above: Diocletian

Above: Constantine I

Above: Julian

Above: Justinian I

POLITICAL EVENTS: AD200–540

AD211 Septimius dies; accession of Caracalla.

212 *Constitutio Antoniniana*: Roman citizenships for all free men.

222 Accession of Alexander Severus.

235 Assassination of Alexander: beginning of the "years of anarchy".

268 Assassination of Gallienus: Zenobia of Palmyra declares independent eastern empire.

270 Accession of Aurelian.

284 Accession of Diocletian: joint rule with Maximian from 286.

303–11 "Great Persecution of Christians".

312 Battle of Milvian Bridge: Constantine defeats Maxentius.

313 Edict of Milan: religious toleration.

324–30 Foundation of Constantinople.

325 Church Council of Nicaea.

337 Death of Constantine; empire divided.

363 Julian killed on Persian campaign.

378 Battle of Adrianople: Valens killed.

386 Removal of Altar of Victory from Senate House; campaign against pagans.

395 Theodosius I dies, dividing empire between Honorius in west, Arcadius in east.

410 Visigoths under Alaric sack Rome.

439 Vandals capture Carthage.

451 Battle of Châlons: Huns defeated by Romans and Visigoths.

476 Last west Roman emperor, Romulus Augustulus, deposed by mercenary Odoacer.

527 Accession of Justinian I in Constantinople.

535 Belisarius begins (East) Roman reconquest of Italy.

Above: Santo Stefano Rotondo, built AD468–83 to house the remains of St Stephen.

CULTURAL EVENTS AD200–540

AD203 Arch of Septimius Severus; extensive building at Lepcis Magna.

216 Baths of Caracalla dedicated.

220s Origen teaching in Alexandria.

250–60s Plotinus, Neoplatonist philosopher, teaching in Rome.

270 Death of Plotinus.

270s Building of Temple of the Sun in Rome.

295–300 Building of Basilica and the Kaiserthermem (imperial baths) at Trier.

298 Construction of Baths of Diocletian starts.

305–6 Diocletian's palace at Split, Croatia.

307–12 Basilica Nova built by Maxentius, completed by Constantine.

c. 310 Birth of poet Ausonius at Bordeaux.

313–23 Building of first Christian basilicas in Rome and Piazza Armerina Villa in Sicily.

350s *Pervigilium veneris* (anon); Woodchester "Great Pavement" mosaic depicting Orpheus.

354 Birth of Augustine, Christian philosopher.

361–3 Julian's *Orations* and *Letters Against the Christians*.

380s Ausonius: *Mosella*.

393 Last Olympic games held in Greece.

413–16 Augustine: *The City of God*.

c. 414 Namatianus writes panegyric of Rome.

430 Death of Augustine in Carthage.

c. 450 Mausoleum of Galla Placidia at Ravenna.

c. 520 Boethius: *The Consolation of Philosophy.*

528–39 Justinian's *Digest of Roman Law* compiled at Constantinople.

529 Justinian closes the Academy at Athens.

532–7 Hagia Sophia built in Constantinople.

Above: A charioteer in his quadriga (four-horse chariot) in Rome c. AD300.

BUILDING THE CITY OF ROME

Rome, notoriously, was not built in a day, nor was it built following any clear-cut plan. Instead, its growth from a few huts above the river Tiber into the world's first giant city was often chaotic. The expanding city was short of space within its walls and spread upwards as well as outwards. Caesar, followed by the emperor Augustus and his successors, tried to plan the city along more rational lines. However, Rome, unlike ancient Alexandria or Antioch – or Paris or Washington today – was never a city of great avenues. Rather, it developed as an accumulation of tight-packed buildings and narrow streets punctuated by such immense monuments as the Colosseum or by noble colonnaded open spaces such as the Forum of Trajan.

Frequently ravaged by fires and serious floods, Rome was constantly rebuilt. The population probably peaked in the 2nd century AD, but emperors continued to adorn Rome lavishly until the time of Constantine. He founded a new centre in the East, Constantinople, which finally eclipsed the old metropolis. Rome's subsequent gradual decay – aggravated more by its inhabitants' tendency to use the ancient buildings as quarries than by barbarian attacks – was slowed by the remarkable skills of the Roman engineers who had built so well. Even the ruins of their ruins still impress.

Left: The Forum Romanum today showing, left to right, the Temple of Castor and Pollux, the Arch of Septimius Severus and, far right, the Curia or Senate House.

BUILDING EARLY ROME:
753–200 BC

Above: This section of the Servian Wall on the Aventine, constructed after the sack of Rome by the Gauls in 390BC, shows the solidity of early Roman buildings.

Below: The impact of Greek classicism after 300BC, such as the early Doric Temple of Neptune in Paestum (built c.500BC and actually dedicated to Hera), was overwhelming in shaping Roman architecture.

The Romans liked to consider themselves superior to their neighbours of central Italy. However, they were deeply influenced in architecture as in other matters by the Etruscans in their early years, whether or not Etruscan kings ever ruled in Rome. The simple shepherds' huts that supposedly sheltered Romulus and other early Romans were devoutly preserved as late as Augustus' time and still survive today. These gave way to larger buildings as Rome became an urban settlement in the 7th century BC.

EARLY CIVIC STRUCTURES

Central to Roman life was the Forum Romanum (market/meeting place), which was first paved in the late 7th century BC. The digging of the *Cloaca Maxima*, the Great Drain or ditch, allowed the draining of the valley of the later Forum Romanum. When covered over, this became and long remained the world's greatest sewer. The first wooden bridge over the Tiber, the *Pons Sublicius*, was built *c.* 600BC, traditionally by the Etruscan king Ancus Marcius. This was the bridge held by Horatio against the Etruscan forces of Lars Porsena in *c.* 505BC, according to the historian Livy. The location of the city was partly dictated by the fact that it provided the lowest practical crossing point of the Tiber. These solidly practical measures sometimes also had a religious aspect, for the word *pontifex*, bridge-maker, came to mean high priest.

ETRUSCAN INFLUENCE

The Etruscans' distinctive form of temple-building deeply influenced the Romans. The Etruscans were also influenced by the Greeks, but unlike Greek temples, whose columns ran all round the *cella* – the central chamber housing the deity's statue – Etruscan temples had their columns chiefly in front, with only a few on the side and none at the back. Etruscan temples also had a staircase at the front, as the temple stood on a high podium. This meant that they could be approached properly only from the front. This suited Etruscan religious practices, which were always much concerned with divination procedures that required their priests to be exactly positioned.

The temple superstructure was built mostly of mud brick, plus a timber or wattle and daub type of construction that was brightly stuccoed or painted, for the area adjacent to Rome lacked easily available attractive building stone. Yellow-grey volcanic *tufa* was the commonest local material, which was later supplemented by travertine stone. Adorning the temples' roofs were similarly colourful life-size terracotta statues of the gods. (Almost all ancient statues and many buildings, whether Greek, Etruscan or Roman, were vividly painted in a way which might strike modern eyes as garish.)

The greatest temple in Rome was that on the Capitoline Hill to Jupiter Optimus Maximus (Best and Greatest), traditionally built by the last Etruscan king Tarquinius Superbus (the Proud) just before his expulsion in 509BC. Raised on a podium about 13ft (4m) high, the huge edifice, 204ft (62m) long and 175ft (53m) long, was comparable in size to the biggest temples of the Greek world and presumably indicative of the wealth of Rome at the time. Only its podium remains intact. This shows the temple was generally Etruscan in style but that it had three *cellae*, with three rows of columns to the front and a single row of seven columns on either side. The central *cella* contained the cult statue of Jupiter – king of the gods and Rome's supreme deity – flanked by shrines to Juno, his wife, to the left, and Minerva (Athena in Greek), his daughter, on the right. The temple burnt down numerous times and was grandiosely rebuilt by Sulla in *c.* 80BC, actually using columns from the Athenian temple to Olympian Zeus but keeping its overall proportions. All private building on the Capitol was banned in 384BC.

Temples were also built around the Forum Romanum. These included the Temple of Saturn *c.* 498BC, the Temple of Castor and Pollux *c.* 483BC and the Temple of Concord of 366BC. A temple to the Greek healing-god Asculepius, whose worship was introduced in 291BC when a plague threatened, was built on the Tiber island. This was outside the *pomerium* or sacred city boundary, for the god, if essential to avert the plague, remained a foreigner.

Following the expulsion of the kings, Rome may for a time have become poorer but the newly republican city continued to grow, with civic life now more focused on the Forum. At first crowded with *tabernae* (shops or booths), the Forum became and remained the grand ceremonial and civic centre of Rome, especially after the cattle and sheep market was moved to the Forum Boarium and the vegetable market was similarly displaced to the

Forum Holitorum. Porticoes and balconies were added to the remaining shops on two sides of the Forum in 318BC, increasing the square's dignity and providing viewing facilities for the people. Many of the city's greatest buildings were rebuilt around the Forum Romanum: the Curia Hostilia (Senate House), the Rostra (Speakers' Platform) from which magistrates could address the people gathered in the *Comitium* (Assembly) and the *Regia* (the house of the Pontifex Maximus).

THE SERVIAN WALL

Among the most imposing structures of early Rome was the Servian Wall, parts of whose massive tufa masonry survive. This was supposedly first built by the Etruscan King Servius in the 6th century BC but was in fact erected in haste only after the Gauls had sacked the nearly defenceless city in 390BC.

Seven miles (11km) long and about 30ft (20m) high, the wall enclosed an area of 1,000 acres (400 ha) and made the city, if properly defended, almost impregnable. It proved its worth against Hannibal, in the Second Punic War (218–202BC), who failed to capture the city.

Above: The remains of the giant columns of the Temple of Vespasian. It was built at the same time (the AD80s) and in the same style as the Temple of Jupiter was rebuilt, but of this almost nothing remains.

Below: The outlet of the Cloaca Maxima, the Great Drain, dug before 600BC in the Etruscan period.

THE LATER REPUBLIC:
200–31BC

Above: The austere Tabularium or Records Office dates from Sulla's dictatorship 82–79BC, but it has a Renaissance upper floor.

As Rome conquered the Mediterranean, it gained numerous artworks looted from Greek cities, especially after 212BC when Syracuse, the greatest Greek city in the West, was captured. Roman generals soon saw other sophisticated Greek cities in the southern and east Mediterranean.

Rome itself now grew rapidly – its population had probably passed the half-million mark before 100BC – and its upper classes grew richer, developing a taste for Greek art, luxury and ostentation. Some Roman nobles began adorning their houses and, more strikingly, their city with statues and buildings that proclaimed their fame, power and wealth while revealing strong Greek influence.

Stone buildings with Ionic or Corinthian columns, such as the white marble Temple of Vesta (actually dedicated to Hercules Victor) of 120BC or the neighbouring Temple of Portunus, built of local stone, must have seemed shockingly innovative in a city still mostly filled with old-fashioned Etruscan-style mud brick and timber buildings.

A DISTINCTIVE ROMAN STYLE

This Greek influence, which was probably at its peak by *c.* 100BC, never completely dominated all aspects of Roman architecture however. The first basilicas, great covered public meeting places such as the Basilica Aemilia of 179BC by the Forum, were essentially Roman buildings, despite their Greek origin and name. Even the Temple of Portunus differs from Greek models in having narrower proportions and a basically Etruscan plan. Most of its columns are massed in front and its side pillars are engaged – half-buried in the wall – a Roman device, decorative rather than structural, that proved very influential in architecture from the Renaissance on. About the same time, the Romans began to realize the potential of the true arch and vault through using *opus caementicum*, Roman concrete. While none of these was a Roman invention – the arch was known in pharaonic Egypt – Romans were to employ all three to unprecedentedly powerful effect.

Perhaps the most impressive surviving structure of the late Republic comes from Praeneste (Palestrina) just outside Rome. Now thought to date from *c.* 130BC, the remarkable complex of the Temple of Fortuna Primigenia, sited 600ft (196m) above the Latium plain, employs a vaulted substructure to support its upper terraces. Behind them the sanctuary of the oracle, novelly semicircular in shape, is cut deep into the hillside. It is approached by a series of criss-crossing ramps and colonnades up which worshippers would have had to walk in increasingly

Below: Dating from c. 120BC, the Temple of Hercules Victor (or Vesta) was one of Rome's first temples to be built in the Greek style and of solid marble.

breathless awe. The whole complex was built of limestone *opus incertum* and was probably originally covered with white stucco to create a marble-like effect which would have gleamed for miles. Such dramatic exploitation of the site suggests a brilliant if unknown architect.

In Rome itself, less radical buildings remained the norm. Of the many works of Sulla, the *Tabularium* (Records Office) of 78BC overlooking the Forum, is one of the few to survive intact (although Michelangelo added an upper floor in the 16th century). A massive, austerely dignified structure well suited to a dictator, it is built mainly of concrete. Its façade is of stone blocks, however, and has the arched opening flanked by columns which was to become a typical Roman feature.

Pompey's huge 55BC theatre in the Campus Martius, outside the ancient *pomerium* (sacred boundary) was the city's first permanent theatre. Theatres had previously been banned on the grounds that they promoted immorality and plays were performed in temporary wooden structures which were subsequently demolished. Pompey's theatre used concrete to support a stone-faced structure on a series of radial and curving vaults, so making a semi-circle 525ft (160m) in diameter that could seat an estimated 27,000 spectators. More than just a theatre, its spacious colonnaded gardens offered art galleries and new open spaces for the Roman public. Recent excavations have shown that a substantial amount of the substructures still survive.

CAESAR'S GRAND PLANS

Never to be outshone by his defeated rival Pompey, Julius Caesar, in control of Rome from 49BC, drafted plans that would have transformed the city into a true rival of the great Hellenistic capitals such as Alexandria or Antioch in splendour as well as size. According to Suetonius, his projects included a "Temple to Mars, the biggest in the world, to build which he would have had to fill up and pave the lake where a naval mock-fight had been staged, and an enormous theatre sloping down from the Tarpeian rock on the Capitoline Hill". (This almost suggests Caesar was planning to create a theatre exploiting a natural slope, on the Greek pattern.) He also planned "The finest possible public libraries", one for Latin, one for Greek literature, a new Curia Julia (Senate House) to replace the old one destroyed in a riot in 52BC, and a wholly new Forum and Basilica. He is also on record as apparently planning to change the course of the Tiber, probably to try to alleviate the flooding problem.

Caesar's assassination in 44BC prevented the full realization of such grand visions. (The land alone for the Basilica Julia in the Forum Romanum reputedly cost 100 million sesterces.) However, his heir Octavian later completed his restored Curia and the Forum and Basilica Julia became the first in a series of imperial basilicas and fora. Rebuilt after yet another fire under Diocletian and stripped of its medieval accretions, the Curia Julia still presents a proudly simple symmetry.

Above: The new Curia, planned by Julius Caesar but built by his heir Octavian, still stands, although it was heavily restored c. AD300.

Below: The Temple of Portunus is Greek in its Ionic columns but reveals an Italian design in its high podium and narrow proportions.

Above: The channels of the Aqua Claudia and Aqua Anio Novus, top right, were carried by the Porta Maggiore, with its rusticated masonry, across two roads. They were completed by Claudius in AD52 to bring water for Rome's growing population.

Below: The Theatre of Marcellus, Rome's largest surviving theatre, dedicated by Augustus in 13BC and named after his first son-in-law, Marcellus.

AUGUSTUS AND HIS HEIRS:
30BC–AD53

According to Suetonius, Augustus claimed he had "found Rome of brick and left it in marble", boasting that he had restored 82 temples in 28BC alone. Even if this boast is exaggerated, it is certainly true that Augustus transformed the city during the half century that he ruled it after 36BC.

CLASSICAL TRANSFORMATION

This Augustan transformation was classical, even conservative in style, at times looking back to 5th century BC Athens for ideas. What made Augustus' boast possible were the new supplies of marble from quarries at Carrara near Lucca. If not as finely translucent as Greek marble, Carrara marble was abundant and relatively cheap. For his grandest buildings, Augustus also imported coloured marble, setting the seal of approval on the use of coloured marble in public building. However, marble façades covered brick and concrete cores, while most housing, especially the tall

Left: Known as the first Roman emperor, Augustus took pains to seem no more than princeps to his contemporaries.

insulae (apartment blocks), lacked marble even to front their flimsy walls of rubble and mud brick. Rome remained extremely vulnerable to fire.

Augustus' first task was to fulfil the grand projects of his adopted father, Caesar, which had been halted by the renewed civil wars after 44BC.

Among these was Caesar's Forum, designed to supplement the old Forum Romanum, Rome's ancient heart. Augustus completed this with fine colonnaded porticoes on three sides and the Temple of Venus Genetrix, the goddess from whom the Julian dynasty claimed descent, on its fourth. He enlarged and completed the great Basilica Julia (aisled hall) to the south of the Forum Romanum, and rebuilt the Curia (Senate House) on the north-east. This now austere building once had a stucco and marble front. Next to it Augustus also restored the Basilica Aemilia, lavishly decorating it with marble. A century later Pliny called it one of Rome's three most beautiful buildings. Augustus redesigned the whole jumbled Forum Romanum, moving the Rostra (Speakers' Platform) to a position at the west end. He built a second rostra at the east end of the Forum in front of the Temple of the Deified Julius Caesar, which he decorated with the ships' prows of Antony's defeated fleet from the Battle of Actium. At the other end was a temple to the now deified Julius and two arches, the Actian Arch (29BC) and the so-called Parthian Arch (19–18BC). This arrangement essentially shaped the Forum until the empire's end.

Greatest of Augustus' own projects was the Forum of Augustus north of the Forum Julium – the extra forum was needed by Rome's ever-growing population. Started in 37BC to celebrate victory over Caesar's assassins, it was only finished in 2BC. It had some markedly Greek features, notably the caryatids (columns like draped women) copied from the Athenian Erechtheum, supporting porticoes on either side on the upper level. Behind this lay *exedrae* (recesses) housing statues of ancient Roman heroes of the Republic, including legendary heroes like Romulus and Aeneas. The new temple of Mars Ultor (Mars the Avenger) was, by contrast, typically Italian. Resting on a high podium and intended to be seen only from the front, its eight tall columns at the front must have dominated the narrow Forum. Behind rose a huge wall built of tufa, which acted as a firewall and hid a slum area known as the Suburra. Augustus' fame as a peace-bringer was honoured by the sublimely classical Ara Pacis (Altar of Peace), whose reliefs show Augustus, his family and friends in solemn but sociable procession. The last temple of Augustus' reign was the Temple of Concord, which again revealed Athenian influences and was probably part-built by Greek craftsmen. Augustus' own house was relatively modest. It consisted of the old house of Hortensius the Orator with other buildings added, such as the House of Livia. However, its location on the Palatine Hill was imperial: he had the mythical Romulus and the god Apollo as his neighbours.

AUGUSTUS' SUCCESSORS

Agrippa, Augustus' right-hand man, inaugurated Rome's tradition of fine public baths with the Baths of Agrippa in the Campus Martius. If modest compared with later bathing palaces, they already had gardens for gymnastics. He built a new bridge, the Pons Agrippae, improved flood defences against the ever-turbulent Tiber and built new warehouses to store grain.

Nearby he constructed the Pantheon (which was later replaced by Hadrian's more famous temple). To satisfy the city's growing water needs, Agrippa built two new aqueducts, the Aqua Julia in 33BC and the Aqua Virgo in 19BC. He did not neglect basics either, reportedly personally inspecting the Cloaca Maxima in a boat – the Great Drain was big enough for such voyages – and restoring it and other sewers.

By comparison, Augustus' successors built little. Tiberius concentrated the whole Praetorian Guard in Rome and necessitated the building of the large rectilinear camp that henceforth abutted the city to accommodate them. He also built himself a big square palace on the Palatine, the Domus Tiberiana.

Gaius Caligula's brief reign (AD37–41) was dominated by such abortive grandiose schemes as a planned new palace and bridge to the Temple of Jupiter from the Palatine Hill. Claudius looked to essentials, on the other hand. His new aqueducts, the Aqua Claudia and Aqua Anio Novus, entered the city on a monumental double arch, the modern Porta Maggiore, whose rusticated stone inspired Renaissance and Neoclassical architects. He also built the marble gates of the Circus Maximus, but his greatest work lay outside Rome, in the new harbour he created north of Ostia at Portus.

Above: The Forum Romanum looking toward the temple of Julius Caesar. Augustus cleared the by then cluttered Forum and gave it what became its definitive shape.

Below: The remains of the Temple of Mars Ultor (Mars the Avenger), Augustus' greatest temple that crowned the Forum of Augustus.

NERO AND THE FLAVIANS:
AD54–96

Above: The Arch of Titus was dedicated to Domitian in AD81 to commemorate the sack of Jerusalem and the apotheosis of his brother Titus, the previous emperor.

Below: The arches of the Amphitheatrum Flavium or Colosseum, the great arena built by the Flavian dynasty and dedicated in AD80. It remains the biggest amphitheatre ever built.

With the accession to the throne of the 16-year-old Nero in AD54 – an emperor passionate about most things Greek and with genuine artistic interests if not talents – Roman architecture entered what is often called its golden age. It lasted until the death of the emperor Hadrian in AD138, himself another noted philhellene (lover of Greek culture).

BUILDING FOR A GOLDEN AGE
As the empire neared its zenith, architects emerged who could use concrete with daring new confidence on lavish imperial projects. Nero's new public baths were complexes which came to include gymnasia, gardens, libraries, restaurants and art galleries as well as swimming pools. Completed in AD62, they were praised by the poet Martial. (The baths were completely rebuilt in the 3rd century AD by the emperor Severus Alexander, along with a new market and a bridge across the Tiber.) However, Nero's real interest lay in extending and extravagantly rebuilding the imperial palace, which was still modest by the standards of the Hellenistic monarchies he admired.

Nero wanted to link the existing palace on the Palatine Hill with the lavish Gardens of Maecenas – already belonging to the emperors – on the Esquiline Hill about 600yds (660m) away. Around AD64 he began building the *Domus Transitoria* (literally Transit Palace) between them. Surviving fragments give some hints of the palace's lavish polychromatic marble, stucco and gilt decorations and also of its radical new architecture.

EFFECTS OF THE GREAT FIRE
The fire that ravaged Rome in AD64 gave Nero the chance to build on a truly titanic scale. He began constructing his Domus Aurea (Golden Palace) on about 300 acres (120ha) of prime central land. This was laid out like a country estate, with extensive grounds and a lake, "like the sea, was surrounded by buildings that resembled cities, and by a landscaped park with ploughed fields, vineyards, pastures and woods," according to Suetonius. The palace amazed contemporaries with marvels such as a dining-room with a revolving ceiling fitted with pipes for sprinkling guests with perfumes. Architecturally, its octagonal room was revolutionary, for it not only broke with all the earlier conventional rectangular plans but exploited the resulting new spatial effects in ways that proved lastingly influential. The architects' concern with the building's interior was something quite new in the Graeco-Roman world.

Nero also issued sensible new building regulations for the ruined capital after the fire. These stipulated wider, straight streets in place of the previous narrow lanes, the building of porticoes to provide fire-fighting platforms, the use of fire-resistant

building materials and a height limit of 70ft (21m) for *insulae* (apartment blocks). These measures were intended to make Rome a safer, more salubrious city. However, they did nothing for Nero's plunging popularity and his reign ended in civil war.

BUILDING FOR THE PEOPLE

Vespasian, the victorious first Flavian emperor (ruled AD69–79), deliberately repudiated Neronian self-indulgence, building for the benefit of the whole Roman people. The wing of the Domus Aurea on the Palatine was incorporated, often at subterranean levels, into the Palatine palace of Domitian and the Esquiline wing of the palace was used by the Flavians as VIP accommodation. Its lake was drained to provide the site for one of the most famous of all Roman buildings: the Flavian Amphitheatre today known as the Colosseum.

The biggest amphitheatre in the empire, the Colosseum could seat up to 45–55,000 people. A vaulted ellipsoid mass rising 159ft (48.5m) to its upper cornice, the building posed unprecedented structural problems. These were solved by skilled engineering that made extensive use of a honeycomb of concrete barrel vaults, although much of the upper structure was of travertine and tufa masonry. The façade is of travertine blocks with purely decorative arches flanked by columns which rise in four successive tiers.

Vespasian also rebuilt the temple to Jupiter on the Capitol which had been destroyed in the civil wars, completed the temple to the deified emperor Claudius that had been left unfinished by Nero and constructed the Forum Pacis (Forum of Peace), to celebrate the return of peace to the empire and to house some of the spoils of the sack of Jerusalem.

Titus, Vespasian's heir, who inaugurated the Colosseum in AD80 with lavish games lasting 100 days, built new baths. According to a 16th-century sketch (for nothing remains) the modest building pioneered the imperial plan for baths with a central bathing block within a large symmetrical enclosure containing gardens and gymnasia. Built of brick-faced concrete, it offered ordinary Romans free or very cheap baths. Titus' brother Domitian (ruled AD81–96), built a fine marble arch in Titus' memory and constructed a vast palace on the Palatine Hill, the Domus Flavia (Flavian Palace). Approaching Nero's in splendour, it became the emperors' main palace from then on and has given us the word palace (from palatine). The palace was made up of a complex of buildings including state apartments, basilica, baths and private rooms. It exploited the use of vaults and was lavishly decorated with coloured and patterned marbles. Domitian, who had become paranoid and reclusive, was assassinated inside his creation in AD96.

Above: The Palatine Palace seen rising above the Circus Maximus. The greatest creation of the despotic emperor Domitian, it became the chief palace of all subsequent Caesars and gave us our word palace.

Below: Nero's Domus Aurea (Golden Palace) was even more renowned for its lavish decorations than its daring architecture. This typical mythological decorative scene shows the birth of Adonis.

TRAJAN AND HADRIAN:
AD98–138

Above: Built as a mausoleum for the emperor Hadrian and his dynasty, the Castel Sant'Angelo became a fort in the Middle Ages. The Ponte Sant'Angelo leading to it also has Hadrianic foundations.

Below: Among the most remarkable of Trajan's many buildings is his market. This covered complex of shops and offices rises above his Forum, with a vaulted hall at its core.

The building of Rome reached its climax under the emperors Trajan (AD98–117) and Hadrian (AD117–38). As the empire neared its confident zenith, the *spolia* (booty) that Trajan gained from conquering Dacia (Romania) helped to pay for his grand projects. The reigns of Trajan and Hadrian also saw the culmination of the so-called Roman revolution in architecture, in which the use of concrete domes and vaults was fully mastered.

TRAJAN'S ROME
Trajan took advantage of a fire that had destroyed the remains of Nero's Domus Aurea in AD104 to start building his baths on part of its site on the Esquiline Hill. Though not the first *thermae* (imperial baths), they were probably three times bigger than those built by Titus, and were almost certainly designed by Apollodorus of Damascus, who was arguably the greatest Roman architect. The baths were orientated to exploit the heat of the afternoon sun in an early form of solar heating and were built of brick-faced concrete. The great

complex, which included gardens, lecture halls, libraries and other rooms for citizens' varied social activities, was dedicated in AD109.

Trajan spent even more money on his Forum and its adjoining Basilica, which were dedicated in AD113. For his Forum, which measured 220 by 130yds (220 by 120m), he cut away the high ground between the Quirinal and Capitoline hills. Flanked by porticoes with marble columns, with a great equestrian statue of Trajan in the centre and large *exedrae* (semicircular recesses) on either side, the Forum became one of the city's wonders. It also provided another much-needed open space for public life in a city whose population was still growing.

On the north-western side of the Forum and instead of the usual temple, Trajan built the Basilica Ulpia (commemorating his family). The largest such public basilica yet built in Rome, it was 185yds (170m) long, with five aisles and apses at either end. Its interior was richly decorated with a marble frieze and columns of grey Egyptian granite, suitably majestic for a building which often served as a law court. Beyond the basilica rose Trajan's Carrara marble column, 125ft (38m) high with a spiral staircase inside. It is carved with a continuous relief vividly illustrating scenes from the recent Dacian wars. Flanking the column were Trajan's two libraries, one for Latin, one for Greek literature, both damp-proofed to protect their vulnerable scrolls. It has been suggested the higher parts of the column's frieze would have been easily visible from the libraries' upper-floor windows, although they are not today.

Behind such obviously opulent buildings rose another more utilitarian but architecturally more radical structure. Trajan's Market was a covered complex built into the hill and remarkable for its

Left: The Pantheon, the Temple of all the Gods, was Hadrian's great architectural statement. Its diameter of 142ft (43.3m) made it the world's broadest unsupported dome for 1700 years after its consecration in AD128.

Below: Recently cleaned so that it looks almost new, Trajan's column is a pillar composed of drums of fine Carrara marble rising 125ft (38m). Originally it had a statue of the emperor on top and held his ashes inside it – a singular honour for the much-loved emperor.

semicircular shape which housed 150 shops and offices. Much of it is still extant, with a great vaulted hall and many booths. The entire market was built of the brick-faced concrete that was now becoming the norm in such complex edifices. Trajan also added a new inner harbour at Portus near Ostia. The hexagonal basin was excavated inland to shelter shipping from the storms that at times made Claudius' older outer harbour unsafe. Its waterfront was lined with warehouses and the basin was connected to the Tiber by a canal.

TEMPLE OF ALL THE GODS

Hadrian, although a more cautious emperor politically (he abandoned Trajan's conquests east of the Euphrates), proved equally radical architecturally. His greatest building was the Pantheon or Temple of all the Gods. Consecrated in AD128, it is often considered the most sublime Roman temple. The temple was revolutionary, for unlike any earlier Roman or Greek temple, the Pantheon was intended to be looked at as much from the inside as the outside. Worshippers stood beneath a perfect hemisphere, its diameter exactly equalling its height, with an *oculus* opening to the heavens above lighting the whole building. The coffered ceiling, which was originally

gilded, was cut back in frame after frame, both a structural and a decorative device. The internal columns were, however, purely decorative, for the weight of the dome is carried by the drum's wall, which is supported by eight giant arches inside the brick-faced concrete walls. With a diameter of 142ft (43.2m) it remained the world's broadest unsupported span until the 19th century.

Hadrian also built the Temple of Venus and Roma to a bold, if perhaps not wholly successful, design. Consecrated in AD135, it was modelled closely on classical Greek precedents and was the first temple in the capital to be built to the cult of Roma. The structure was probably built to Hadrian's own designs. It had two *cellae* (inner chambers) which backed on to each other. Like Greek temples, it had columns all round, resting not on a Roman podium but merely on top of steps, which meant that it did not rise clear above its surroundings.

Hadrian also built a mausoleum for himself and his dynasty across the Tiber. This circular building of marble-faced tufa and concrete originally had earth piled high on it but has since become the Castel Sant'Angelo. Hadrian also built the bridge leading to it, the Pons Aelius.

ROME IN THE LATER EMPIRE:
AD138–312

Above: Coin of Marcus Aurelius, emperor AD161–80 who built Rome's second great commemorative column.

Below: The Arch of Constantine, built AD315 by the emperor who started Rome's conversion to Christianity and founded a new capital in the east. His arch, however, is oddly conservative, stealing earlier edifices' decorative figures.

The 60 years following Hadrian's death saw relatively little building in Rome. This was due in part to the exhausting wars that filled most of Marcus Aurelius' reign between AD161–80.

The emperor Antoninus Pius built a temple to the deified Hadrian and another to his wife Faustina (and later his deified self) in AD141 in the Forum Romanum. The temple, now embedded in a later building on the Campus Martius, owes its excellent state of preservation to its conversion into a church, a fate that saved it from being plundered for building materials but which relatively few ancient buildings experienced.

Marcus also began construction of a column commemorating his Danubian wars, which consciously echoed that of Trajan. Completed under his son Commodus, its carvings reveal the sea-change that was beginning to affect Graeco-Roman art. Classical realism had begun to give way to a more stylized portrayal of characters and to much starker and more realistic depictions of war.

With the advent of the new Severan dynasty in AD193 came new ambitions. Septimius Severus added a new wing to the Palatine palace and built more *thermae* (public baths), but these were soon utterly surpassed by those built by his son, Caracalla (ruled AD211–17), the bare ruins of which are still overwhelming today. The *Thermae Antoninianae* or Baths of Caracalla followed Trajan's Baths' layout of a century earlier but on a far larger scale. The whole complex with its gardens and gymnasia was nearly 500yds (460m) square and enclosed an area of almost 50 acres (20ha). Revealing the new priorities of Roman architects, the baths had luxuriously decorated interiors but rather plain exteriors.

EASTERN INFLUENCE
The Severans also built temples, mainly to eastern deities – Caracalla to Serapis, Elagabalus (ruled AD218–22) to Baal and Alexander Severus (ruled AD222–35) to Isis, although this last was essentially a restoration. The influx of Eastern gods reflected the growth of new religions in the population as well as the emperors' own personal preferences. Elagabalus, for example, had been a priest of the cult of Baal in Syria. On a microscopic scale, a detailed map of Rome, known today as the *Forma Urbis Romae* and dated AD205–8, was carved on 151 pieces of marble, under Septimius Severus. The map's few surviving fragments are invaluable for our knowledge of the ancient city.

ROME REWALLED
The catastrophes of the 3rd century AD, when more than 30 rival emperors fought each other in the 50 years after AD235, led to opportunistic barbarian invasions across the empire. This spelt a temporary end to massive but non-essential projects. Rome itself came under threat of barbarian

attack for the first time in almost 400 years. To counter this, new walls were constructed in great haste by the emperor Aurelian (ruled AD270–5), for the Servian walls had long since been allowed to decay. The new walls incorporated existing structures such as the aqueduct of Claudius (now the Porta Maggiore) and the Praetorian Guards' camp. Built of brick-faced concrete, 25ft (7.2m) high with 18 gates and 381 towers, they ran for 12 miles (19.3km) and covered an area of almost 3,500 acres (1,400ha), which was by then the extent of the city. Strengthened by both Maxentius and Valentinian I in the 4th century and Honorius in the early 5th, they protected Rome, often inadequately, up to 1870 when the city was incorporated into a reunited Italy. Aurelian also built a Temple to Sol Invictus (the Unconquered Sun).

ORDER RESTORED

Diocletian, founder of the tetrarchy system of four co-emperors, restored order to the empire during his reign (AD284–305). He rebuilt the Curia (Senate House), together with the two temples of Saturn and Vesta, reorganized the cluttered Forum Romanum and built another set of baths even grander than Caracalla's. Completed

in AD305, the huge size of the baths – they measure 785 by 475ft (240 by 144m) – can be judged today by the 16th century church of Santa Maria degli Angeli that Michelangelo built in the *frigidarium* (cold bath). Diocletian and his fellow tetrarchs, however, no longer ruled the empire from Rome, but chose other cities closer to the endangered frontiers as their capitals.

Maxentius (ruled AD306–12) was the last effective emperor to make Rome his capital, although he ruled only part of the Western empire. Appropriately, he adorned the city with its grandest basilica, the Basilica Nova (which was actually completed by Constantine). The basilica's massive structure – rising to 115ft (35m) with a central nave of 260 by 80ft (80 by 25m) flanked by huge *exedrae* – recalls the greatest *thermae*. Maxentius also built a new palace or villa on the Via Appia, complete with a circus and race track.

After Maxentius' defeat, the victorious Constantine built a grand triple arch in AD315, plundering sculptures from earlier monuments for this age saw little new sculpture, and built Rome's last great *thermae* in AD320. Such buildings perpetuated Rome's proudly pagan imperial traditions but Constantine is chiefly noted for his patronage of Christianity.

Above: Ruins of the Basilica Nova, Rome's largest basilica, started by the emperor Maxentius and completed by his victorious rival Constantine after AD312.

Below: Aerial view of the Baths of Caracalla, built AD211–17, which enclosed an area of 50 acres (20ha) with gardens, gymansia and restaurants besides the actual baths themselves.

BUILDING TECHNIQUES AND STYLES

Roman buildings often seem to emulate classical Greek models, most notably in their use of classical columns. However, Roman architecture soon developed its own dynamic, versatile and highly practical form of classicism. This employed arches, vaults and domes, all made possible by the Romans' exploitation of concrete. The Romans developed types of *opus caementicum* (concrete) early on, due to a relative lack of attractive, readily accessible stone and also to their desire to build fast. They had abundant tufa, soft volcanic rock of varying densities and, further afield, travertine, a fine but brittle limestone. Only with the opening of marble quarries near Carrara in the 40s BC did relatively cheap white marble reach Rome. Most buildings were concrete structures, brick-faced then covered with marble, stucco or plaster.

Although classical columns or pediments in Roman buildings often had no load-bearing function, they were long thought essential to dignify and humanize buildings. However, in the 3rd century AD fashions changed. Although the exteriors of buildings still had some decoration, they became secondary as architects began concentrating mostly on interiors. As most such decorations have vanished, Roman buildings can look far more austere than they did when originally built.

Left: The bridge at Alcantara, Spain, built under Trajan (AD98–117) and still in use, demonstrates Roman engineering skills at their most inspiring and durable.

BUILDING MATERIALS

Above: Opus incertum, the first type of facing for Roman concrete, consisted of irregular-shaped small stones placed on a concrete core.

Above: Opus reticulatum, the next type of facing for concrete, had small square-faced stones laid diagonally creating a network of interconnecting lozenge-shaped joints.

Above: Opus testaceum, the third sort of facing for concrete, had brick or tile facing over a rubble or concrete core.

Right: The main body of the Pantheon is of brick-faced concrete. The giant portico had 16 grey and red Egyptian granite columns weighing 84 tons each, and the pediment was of white marble.

The earliest building materials used in the city of Rome were mud brick and timber-framing. However, soft volcanic tufa was used for some structures, most notably for the Servian Walls (built *c.* 378BC). Well-suited for the older type of *domus* (one-storied detached house), timber-framed mud brick continued as a common building material in the more jerry-built multi-storey *insulae* (apartment blocks) built from the end of the 3rd century BC. These were built, despite obvious structural weakness, at least until the great fire of AD64. This led to new, although not universally observed, building regulations that encouraged gradual improvements in the quality of *insulae*.

ANCIENT CONCRETE

Using a characteristic trial and error approach, Romans learnt to exploit other materials, especially *opus caementicum*, their own type of concrete. At times this pragmatic approach worked wonders as at Praeneste, whose vaults still stand.

Perhaps inspired by examples from Pompeii, the Romans in the 3rd century BC began building walls using mortar made of lime and *pozzolana* – black volcanic sand first found near Puteoli (Pozzuoli). The walls' cores were filled with smallish stones which produced a solid, cohesive mass when mortar was laid on top. Rome had abundant supplies of limestone which could be burnt to produce lime, essential to lime mortar. Vitruvius, the architect and theorist writing *c.* 30BC, recommended three parts of volcanic sand to one of mortar.

Roman concrete was seldom poured like modern concrete, but was normally laid by hand in roughly horizontal courses between timber frames. These were left in place and mortar added to produce a very strong monolithic whole.

In effect, Roman *opus caementicum* was an artificial stone, vastly cheaper and more malleable than any from a quarry. Initially Roman concrete used for building walls was faced with *opus incertum*, a surface of

irregularly placed, small stones over the concrete core. The Porticus Aemilia, begun in 193BC, used this concrete on a large scale for its rows of barrel-vaults. *Opus reticulatum*, which succeeded this early concrete, had small stones with a square face laid diagonally to create a network of interconnected lozenge-shaped joints. This facing technique was developed in Rome and used to build the Theatre of Pompey. Completed in 55BC, this was Rome's first large permanent theatre. The third and final sort of concrete was *opus testaceum*, that had a brick or tile facing over its rubble and mortar core. By Augustus' reign, the Romans were increasingly using red *pozzolana* which produced a finer, stronger cement. (The Romans never made the mistake, common in the mid-20th century, of leaving bare concrete walls exposed to the elements, where rain could soon disfigure them.)

STANDARDIZED BRICKS
When Augustus boasted that he had found Rome a city of brick and left it a city of marble, he may have been thinking of a city made of mud brick, but fired bricks were becoming more common as building materials. The Theatre of Marcellus – planned by Caesar and completed by Augustus by 13BC – is partly built of a reddish-yellow brick, lightly baked to absorb mortar porously.

Standardized bricks offer builders obvious advantages and Roman bricks came in four main sizes: *bessalis* eight Roman inches square (20cm); *pedalis* one Roman foot square (30cm); *sesquipedalis* 18 Roman inches square (45cm); and *bipedalis* two Roman feet square (60cm). These bricks were often cut into triangles to face walls and into rectangles to face arches. *Bessales* were the bricks most commonly used in the Principate; Domitian's giant Palatine Palace required a lot of *bipedales* for brick facing. *Bessales* were often used for the *pilae* of a hypocaust, and *bipedales* were used to span the distance between *pilae* as well as for bonding courses in concrete

Right: The obelisk in the fountain in the Piazza Navona in Rome (by Bernini, c. 1650) was imported by Domitian for the Temple of Isis he built in the Campus Martius.

walls. Bricks were made along the Tiber valley and transported by barge when possible. Roof tiles, which were hard-baked for waterproofing and darkish red in colour, sometimes had their flanges cut off for use for building purposes. Both tiles and bricks were occasionally stamped with the name of the *figulus* (brick-maker) and with the names of that year's consuls, a common Roman dating method. Travertine stone quarried near Tivoli was also used for structural purposes under the emperors, for example in the Colosseum.

IMPERIAL IMPORTS
Rome imported both finished artworks and building materials on an increasingly large scale. Some victorious nobles in the last century of the Republic used Greek marble to adorn the temples proclaiming their own or their families' genius. Sulla the dictator went further, grabbing giant Corinthian columns from the unfinished Temple of the Olympian Zeus in Athens to rebuild the great Temple of Jupiter on the Capitol in 82BC. (The two gods were by then effectively identical, so the theft was less sacrilegious than it might seem.) Supplementing new supplies of white marble from Carrara, Augustus began importing coloured marbles from the Aegean, Asia Minor and North Africa for his buildings. Coloured marble had been thought decadent before, but there was nothing decadent about Augustus.

Egypt, his greatest conquest, provided another source of building materials and artefacts, notably obelisks. In 10BC Augustus erected Rome's first obelisk, a sundial in the Piazza di Montecitorio. Gaius Caligula imported another, larger, obelisk in a specially constructed ship. In the Piazza Navona today stands an obelisk originally brought to Rome by the emperor Domitian (ruled AD81–96) for the sanctuary of the Egyptian goddess Isis.

Below: Four comparative Roman brick sizes: bessalis, 8 Roman inches square (20cm); pedalis, 1 Roman foot square (30cm); sesquipedalis, 18 Roman inches square (45cm); and bipedalis, two Roman feet square (60cm).

VAULTS, ARCHES, DOMES

Above: The Pantheon's perfect dome remained unsurpassed in span for 1700 years.

Below: In Trajan's Market the Romans made highly practical use of the arch and vault.

The chief characteristic of Roman architecture from a relatively early date was its use of vaults, arches and domes. The buildings so created, especially during Nero's reign (AD54–68) and after, were still often adorned by classically proportioned columns, but they were not usually structurally dependent on such pillars. Instead, vaults, arches and domes transmitted their weight to the supporting walls.

AN ARCHITECTURAL REVOLUTION

This development marked a true revolution in architecture, though one that was unplanned and untheoretical, for Roman architects and builders (there was little difference in practice) discovered the basic principles of engineering through trial and error. A vault is essentially an elongated arch covering a space. Built of brick, concrete, stone or any masonry building material, like an arch it depends on materials supporting each other under pressure.

The simplest vault is a barrel or tunnel vault, the continuation of the semicircular section covered by an arch. A cross- or groin vault is created when two barrel vaults intersect at right angles, producing what looks superficially like a dome. A cloister, domical or pavilion vault derives from the intersection of two barrel vaults, so that it rises from a square or polygonal base to create a dome-like structure. The Tabularium or Records Office (built 82–78BC to Sulla's orders) employs cross-vaults in its lower floors.

ARCHES

A stone or brick arch consists of wedge-shaped blocks (called arch-stones or voussoirs) that stay in place because of the mutual pressure of one stone upon another. These are arranged in a curve to span an opening and to support the often vast weight on top, acting in place of a horizontal lintel (beam).

Stone is normally strong under pressure but weak under tension. This means lintels, lengths of extended stone, cannot span large distances while arches can. Each wedge-shaped voussoir, which is wider at its top than its bottom, cannot fall even if the arch is almost flat, as some are in the Colosseum, for example. However, arches need support until the keystone is in place, so construction of an arch usually requires a timber framework, called centring, to support it while it is being built.

The most distinctive Roman arches are their triumphal arches, which proclaim their engineers' skills as clearly as those of the emperors they commemorate. However, invisible interior arches support many Roman buildings.

TRUE DOMES

A dome is a form of vault, composed of semicircular or segmental sections raised on a circular, elliptical, square or polygonal base. If built on a square base, an intermediate piece needs to be added for the transition between the square and the circle. It took Roman architects a long time to learn to build true domes. Even in the Baths of Caracalla, completed *c.* AD218, the architects were still experimenting.

Central to the dome's development is the extant Octagonal Room in Nero's Domus Aurea (Golden Palace), the grandiose palace he had constructed after the fire of AD64. Little is known about either Severus or Celer, the designer and engineer behind this great (and speedily executed) project. Whether their work represents a revolution or merely an evolution remains debatable, but their ingenuity, amounting almost to genius, in overcoming the problems in the Domus Aurea is indisputable. Standing on eight brick-faced concrete piers, which were originally lavishly covered in marble and stucco, this dome begins as an eight-sided domical vault but becomes a true dome towards the top. It has a wide *oculus* (central opening) to admit light, supplemented by other light wells.

With the Pantheon, built under Hadrian (ruled AD117–38), the problems of building a vast but perfect dome had finally been solved. This was perhaps due to the genius of its probable architect Apollodorus. Both the diameter and the height of its rotunda (cylinder-shaped building) of brick-faced concrete are identical at 140ft (43.2m). Eight piers support eight arches running right through the walls and help to buttress the walls against the outward thrust of the dome. The dome's weight was reduced by coffering (panels sunk in the dome),

Right: The triple Arch of Septimius Severus reveals the Romans as masters of arch-building.

producing an effect which is at once decorative and structural and one which has been much copied in recent centuries. The lightest forms of pumice were used along with concrete in the upper dome to reduce the overall weight.

To reduce the weight of the upper parts of vaults or domes further, *amphorae* (earthenware jars) were later used in the upper parts of some domes, such as the Mausoleum of Constantia (now the Church of Santa Constanza). This allowed windows to be inserted in the dome. The church, though still Roman, points towards Byzantine architecture, whose archetypal achievement would be the dome of the cathedral of Hagia Sophia. The dome of that great cathedral in Constantinople built by the Emperor Justinian in the 6th century AD, seems to sail effortlessly above its square basis, marking both the culmination and the last chapter of Roman architecture.

Above: The barrel or tunnel vault is the simplest form of vault, continuing the semi-circular section of an arch.

Above: The groin vault, very popular with the Romans, is formed by two identical barrel vaults intersecting at 90 degrees.

BUILDING PRACTICES AND TECHNIQUES

The Roman genius at organizing and controlling huge numbers of men was as dramatically demonstrated in the ways they mobilized labour to erect vast public buildings as in their deployment of large standing armies.

MASS MOBILIZATION

There was nothing original about mass mobilization in itself. All pre-industrial societies used huge numbers of labourers for their grand projects, from the Egyptian pyramids up to the 19th century.

What is remarkable about so many of the great imperial edifices, especially in Rome, is the *speed* with which they were erected. Nero's huge Domus Aurea (Golden Palace), for example, was built in only four years after the great fire of AD64. The Colosseum, a far more solidly built and enduring structure, took only a decade (AD70–80) to complete between its conception and its lavish inauguration (although its topmost tier may not have been completed until the reign of Domitian). The immense complex of the Baths of Caracalla apparently took only six years to build in its entirety from AD211. By comparison, some cathedrals in medieval Europe took literally centuries to conceive, design and build.

The Romans usually built fast but they seldom built shoddily, at least for public buildings. Indeed, they built to last. They also built without the aid of any mechanical power – without even the wheelbarrow, as far as we know. The closest they got to any mechanization was the treadmill illustrated in the funerary sculpture of the Haterii family from the late Flavian period (AD69–96). This shows five men turning a great "squirrel cage" at the bottom of a large crane to lift blocks up to a temple building site.

More typical of small-scale Roman building methods is the scene from the 4th-century AD Tomb of Trebius Justus in Ostia. This shows two men on scaffolding laying bricks, two men bringing mortar and bricks up the ladder and another mixing mortar on the ground with a hoe, a sight that must have been common across the empire.

SKILLED LABOUR

Although Roman architects lacked the celebrity status some enjoy today, Vitruvius gave stringent requirements for the (ideal) architect. He was expected to be "literate, a skilled draughtsman and good at geometry, well-versed in history and philosophy, knowledgeable about music, medicine and law, with experience in astronomy". Although not every architect could have had these qualifications, almost all would have been able to draw and make accurate models. We know little about even the most famous Roman architects, such as Rabirius under Domitian and Apollodorus under Trajan.

Unknown master carpenters played an almost equally vital role in making the centring or framework essential in erecting domes, arches and vaults. They had to produce accurate models, for a dome or vault's centring required a continuous surface. This gave the dome its shape

Above: The empire's largest amphitheatre, the Colosseum, took only 10 years to build (AD70–80) but still stands, in parts almost intact.

Below: The tomb of Trebius Justus from the 4th century AD shows a typical small firm of Roman builders at work, perhaps with slaves working alongside free labourers.

while supporting the weight of the *opus caementicum* (concrete) that was laid on it. To reduce the huge amount of wood needed for *centring*, large roof tiles comparable in size to *bessales* or *bipedales* were later sometimes laid across timber scaffolding instead of solid timber planking. When the concrete had set, the timbers could be removed.

A big advantage of *opus caementicum* was that it required far less skilled labour than the masons who cut and laid stone. Even so, many Romans were employed in the building trade – possibly as many as 20,000 during the great imperial projects. The construction of the Baths of Caracalla is thought to have employed about 10,000 men at its peak, including about 700 marble workers and 500 decorators. Many of these would not have been slaves; the millionaire property-developer Crassus (died 53BC), who reputedly owned a team of 500 slave architects and labourers, was the exception rather than the norm.

Most building teams would have been made up of less than a dozen men: the boss, some free labourers and a handful of slaves. Building contractors normally belonged to a guild or trade union, the *collegium fabrum tignuariorum*, which had 1330 members in the 2nd century AD, mostly men of modest means. The *collegium* was divided with almost military precision into 60 *decuriae*, each with its own officials. When someone reputedly suggested a labour-saving device for the building trade to the emperor Vespasian (AD69–79), he rewarded the inventor but rejected his idea, saying he could not deprive the Roman people of work.

SUPPLYING MATERIALS

Such huge projects required prodigious supplies of raw materials. By the end of the 1st century AD, huge amounts of marble, granite and porphyry were being imported into Rome. Exotic imports included Egyptian granite and Aegean coloured marble, but most material came from much closer to Rome. About 100,000 poles would have been needed for the scaffolding alone of the

Baths of Caracalla. Vast quantities of tufa or limestone were excavated; 100,000 cubic metres of material were needed for the Colosseum alone. Much of this was travertine for the façade and load-bearing piers, but a lot of concrete was also used, of which the chief source was the quarries near Tivoli.

As there was no waterway connecting these quarries with Rome, all the stone must have been transported in ox-carts. It has been suggested that one heavily laden cart must, on average, have left the Tivoli quarries every few minutes for 400 years. Sea transport could also have been used to ship stone from limestone quarries on the coast at Terracina. Increasingly under the empire, raw materials were stockpiled in warehouses by the Tiber for use in later projects.

Above: The Tomb of the Haterii, a wealthy family of builders c. AD90, showing a crane being used to lift blocks of stone in a squirrel cage up a construction site. This simple, small-scale machine was typical of Roman technology, which advanced only very modestly. Most teams of builders were quite small, although the total work force employed in the great projects such as the imperial baths must have run to tens of thousands.

PUBLIC BUILDINGS

Although most people in the Roman empire lived and worked on the land, city life was considered the only really civilized life, ideally passed in Rome itself. Emperors decorated the imperial city with ever more monuments and buildings – baths, arches, fountains, temples, palaces, libraries, basilicas, fora – until Rome itself became the greatest wonder of the ancient world. The emperor Constantius II, visiting Rome for the first time in AD357, was "thunder-struck" to see "baths built like provinces, the great solid mass of the amphitheatre ... so tall that human sight can scarcely reach its top".

Such majestic buildings were replicated in hundreds of cities around the empire that were built or partly rebuilt in the Roman style by their inhabitants. Urban life, which was mostly lived in the open, focused on the Forum (market/ meeting place). This was a key public space in any Roman city and it was copied across the empire. Life in the open suited a Mediterranean people whose homes were often cramped. However, as Rome became richer, more spacious buildings – most notably the grand imperial baths, along with libraries and basilicas – provided covered, sometimes heated shelter for commercial and legal activities. This was appreciated not only in more northerly cities of the empire such as Lyons, London or Trier but also in Rome itself, where winters can be chilly and wet.

Left: The Forum Romanum in the 19th century. The heart of Rome from very early days, the Forum was replicated in almost every city founded by the Romans across the empire.

THE FORUM ROMANUM

Above: Under Julius Caesar, who ruled Rome for five years after 49BC, the Forum Romanum was extensively replanned, although little was actually built.

For the Romans, the word forum meant a meeting place, a public area and a market place. The original Forum Romanum, a marshy area between the Capitoline and Palatine Hills, was drained and paved by the 6th century BC. Long before the expulsion of the kings, traditionally in 509BC, this area became the centre of the city's social and political life.

LIFE IN THE FORUM

On the north-west side of the Forum stood the old Senate House, the Curia Hostilia. In the roughly circular space in front of the Curia the people met in the Comitia (Assembly) to exercise their (strictly limited) powers of voting. From the Rostra, the platform adorned with the prows of galleys captured at the Battle of Antium in 338BC, magistrates and candidates for magistracy orated and harangued the people. So, more rarely, did some of the less autocratic emperors later.

In the Forum Romanum, great nobles met their *clientalia*, supporters or hangers-on. Business (*negotium*) and other deals were made among more general socializing. The

Below: To accommodate Rome's swelling population, Augustus constructed a Forum bearing his name just to the north of the Forum Romanum. It was dominated by the Temple of Mars Ultor, three of whose columns still stand.

custom was that business was conducted in the Forum Romanum in the morning. Meetings for pleasure took place later in the day and elsewhere in the city. Augustus tried to enforce the wearing of the traditional, rather cumbersome formal toga in the Forum, instead of the more casual Greek-style *chiton*, in order to preserve the Forum's special dignity.

Initially, shops or booths (*tabernae*) lined the Forum's north-east and south-west sides, leaving only two sides for public buildings. As Rome grew explosively through the late Republic and early Principate – its population, at least 200,000 in 200BC, more than doubled in the following century before doubling again in the next – other fora became necessary. Rome's emperors provided these with increasing lavishness.

In the early Republic (500–250BC) the Forum Romanum must have still seemed half-rustic with its cattle and vegetable markets. Only a few temples such as those of Saturn or Castor and Pollux added a note of Roman *dignitas* (dignity). This was not inappropriate in what was still predominantly a city of farmer-citizens. (In 458BC, for example, Regulus was called from his plough to save the city in a moment of acute danger but then happily returned to his fields.) However, when the markets were removed in 318BC and porticoes added to the shops, the Forum began to acquire the majesty better suited to the city which was fast becoming the greatest in Italy.

Chief among Rome's new ennobling edifices were the basilicas. These large, aisled buildings were used for both commercial and legal affairs. The Basilica Aemilia, which was built on the north-east side of the Forum and completed by *c.* 170BC, had three aisles and three floors. To the north-west of the Forum, Sulla, dictator from 82 to 79BC, built the grimly

imposing Tabularium (Records Office) on the slopes of the Capitoline, rebuilt the Curia and raised the overall level of the Forum by about 3ft (1m), paving it with marble and tidying up its edges. However, none of these works increased the area of the now overcrowded Forum itself and indeed, they tended to reduce it.

CAESAR AND AUGUSTUS

Julius Caesar's plans for reorganizing the Forum Romanum were typically ambitious and, equally typically, were left unfulfilled at the time of his assassination in 44BC. He ordered the rebuilding of the Curia (Senate House) that had been burnt down again in a riot in 52BC. Henceforth, the Senate House was always known as the Curia Julia. In place of the old Basilica Sempronia, Caesar built a new larger basilica, the Basilica Julia.

Although he settled a reported 80,000 Roman citizens in colonies outside Italy, Caesar realized that radical measures were needed to deal with Rome's growing demand for public space. He therefore spent 100 million sesterces on new land for a brand new centre for Rome: the Forum of Julius Caesar to the north-east of the Forum Romanum. He did not live to see the completion of any of his plans.

Caesar's heir Octavian, later Augustus, had the time, money and authority to fulfil them all and gave the Forum Romanum the shape it retained for most of the rest of the empire. Besides completing the Basilica Julia and the new Curia, Augustus tidied up the whole Forum, which had become encumbered with many monuments over the years, erected by the city's great nobles. He moved the Rostra to the north-west end of the open area of the Forum to provide an axial focus and built a temple to his now deified predecessor at the opposite end. This was dedicated in 29BC, with another rostra in front of it, decorated with prows from his victory over Antony and Cleopatra at Actium.

Beside the new rostra were Augustus' own triumphal arches; the Actian Arch (erected in 29BC) and the Parthian Arch (erected in 19–18BC), which listed all the triumphs celebrated, from Romulus down to the last to be celebrated by a general not of the imperial family, that of Cornelius Balbus in 19BC. When the Basilica Aemilia burnt down after a fire in 14BC, Augustus had it rebuilt in a much more lavish style.

Above: Much the grandest new forum built by any of the emperors was that of Trajan who, flushed with victory over the Dacians and unprecedentedly wealthy, in AD107 ordered the construction of an enormous piazza 220 by 130 yds (200 by 120m), flanked by two semi-circular exedra. There was a resplendent equestrian (mounted) statue of the emperor in the middle of the court. To the right lay the Forum of Augustus and, below it, the smaller Forum of Julius Caesar. Trajan's Column still rises up on the left between what were his two libraries, one for Greek and one for Latin literature.

THE IMPERIAL FORUM

Above: Coin of Augustus, whose officially acknowledged reign started in 27BC but who had already started remodelling Rome by carrying out some of Caesar's grand projects in honour of his adopted and deified father.

In no other building project did Caesar show himself so boldly radical as in proposing a wholly new forum for Rome, but it was arguably a long overdue decision. The original Forum, while adequate for a relatively small citizen body, was not big enough for the huge numbers who now crowded the imperial city. An Augustan census counted 350,000 male citizens in Rome. Although it is not likely all of them were resident in the city itself and that this number included boys over the age of ten, this was still a huge population. The series of imperial fora that came to supplement (never to displace) the old Forum gave the metropolis vital extra public space, besides allowing emperors and their architects opportunities to shine.

LEGENDARY STANDING

Caesar's Forum had colonnades round three sides. At one end was a temple to the goddess Venus Genetrix, the mother of Aeneas, the legendary ancestor of Romulus and Remus who founded Rome and from whom the Julian family claimed descent. Augustus followed this pattern

for his own Forum just to the north-east. Begun in 37BC, it was only completed in 2BC, an unusually long time for normally speedy Roman builders, as Augustus liked to joke. It was dominated by the Temple of Mars Ultor (Mars the Avenger) which celebrates the victory over Caesar's assassins at Philippi in 42BC.

Inside the temple were statues of Mars, Venus and the deified Caesar, with the standards of the legions lost to the Parthians at Carrhae but restored after the eastern settlement of 19BC. The temple rises abruptly from the Forum's rather narrow space. According to Suetonius, Augustus had wanted to buy more land than he finally did and, perhaps as a result, the Forum is not wholly symmetrical. This was disguised by the flanking porticoes. Massive walls of tufa 115ft (35m) high served as a firebreak and shielded the complex from the crowded *insulae* area of Suburba just beyond. The temple shows Hellenistic classicism in the decorations mingled with Italian architectural traditions. Greek craftsmen probably carved the caryatids (stone female figures supporting an entablature) on the upper floor of the porticoes and the capitals of the columns and pilasters but the plan is very Roman. On each side, semicircular *exedrae* (recesses) housed statues of legendary and historical figures including Romulus and Aeneas and earlier Julians and emphasized the legitimacy of the Augustan settlement. The years of building the Forum also saw the appearance of Virgil's epic poem *The Aeneid*, which gave the new regime the legendary justification which it craved.

No other Julio-Claudian emperor added a forum. However, Vespasian, first of the succeeding Flavians, added the Forum Pacis (Forum of Peace), which was built just to the east between AD71–9. Dominated by its Temple of Peace, it was

Below: The commercial activities that had once taken place in the Forum Romanum found a new home in the covered Markets of Trajan that curved dramatically above Trajan's Forum.

meant to emphasize the blessings of peace restored after the horrors of civil war – which were very real, including fighting in Rome itself – and to celebrate the capture of Jerusalem in AD70 by Titus, Vespasian's son.

A rectangle 120 by 150yds (110 by 135m), laid out on the same alignment as Augustus', the forum was occupied mostly by a formal garden which was enclosed on three sides with porticoes whose columns were of red Egyptian granite. The fourth side had a colonnade of large marble columns. The temple façade's six columns were in line with the surrounding columns, so the temple did not dominate the complex. It contained famous trophies such as the Seven-branched Candlestick and Ark of the Covenant from Jerusalem (spoils of war), as well as fine Greek paintings and sculptures. Pliny praised it as one of the three most beautiful buildings in Rome; the others were the Basilica Aemilia and the Forum of Augustus. The short reign of Nerva (AD96–98) saw the completion of the small Forum Transitorium which had been started by Domitian. This linked up the previously disparate series of fora.

TRAJAN'S FORUM

The last and grandest imperial forum was that of Trajan, the greatest imperial builder since Augustus. Flush with gold from his conquest of Dacia, Trajan in AD107 ordered the construction of a vast piazza 220 by 130yds (200 by 120m), flanked by two semicircular *exedrae*. To allow this, the high ground between the Esquiline and Capitoline Hills had to be cut back to a depth of up to 125ft (38m). Inspired by Augustus' Forum and entered through a colonnaded sunken atrium, the Forum had at its centre a huge gilded equestrian statue of Trajan. The upper floors of the colonnades, lined with gigantic marble

Right: This map reveals the intense concentration of public buildings in a relatively small area around the ancient Forum Romanum.

columns, had statues of captive Dacians and horses. The entrance side of the Forum was gently curved. At the far end, instead of a temple, rose the huge Basilica Ulpia with libraries beyond, and beyond that, Trajan's column, which is still intact. The covered complex of booths called Trajan's Markets, which rises up the hill behind in a series of vaulted galleys and halls, also survives.

Above: Despite the many new imperial fora, the Forum Romanum continued to be adorned with new and restored temples including that of the posthumously deified Vespasian. His reign (AD69–79) marked the start of the new Flavian dynasty who proved dramatic builders.

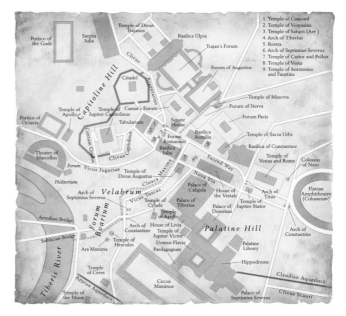

ROME'S BASILICAS AND THE SENATE HOUSE

Above: Constantine I (AD306–37) was the last emperor to erect great buildings in Rome, although he finally founded a new capital on the Bosphorus.

Below: Some of the ruins of the enormous Basilica Julia. Once one of Rome's grandest basilicas, it was actually built by Augustus and was the place where law courts sat.

The largest public buildings in Rome, except for the grand imperial baths, were the basilicas. Oblong halls on one or two floors, they sometimes had clerestory lighting and some of the larger basilicas had double colonnades and apses (semi-circular recesses) at the end. They were originally used as covered extensions to the forum and later became law courts, exchanges and assembly halls. The word "basilica" may derive from the Greek for royal hall, but the concept was typically adopted and developed by the Romans and later exported across the empire.

A NEW PUBLIC SPACE

The first basilica was built on land bought by Cato the Censor after one of Rome's many fires had destroyed buildings round the north-east of the Forum Romanum *c.* 180BC. This basilica, the Basilica Aemilia, named after Aemilius Lepidus who helped supervise its construction, soon faced another, the Basilica Sempronia which was built in 169BC by Tiberius Sempronius Gracchus, the father of

the radical Gracchi brothers. Houses belonging to nobles like the Scipios were demolished to make way for it. Both halls were surrounded by porticoes, from which spectators could watch both the Forum's civic life and the gladiatorial games sometimes staged there, and by *tabernae*. Very little remains of them, but they were probably built of local tufa stone. Their function was initially to shelter businessmen and the general public. Only gradually did the proceedings of law courts move inside them, when the halls were subdivided by curtains.

Caesar planned a larger and more splendid basilica, the Basilica Julia, to replace the Sempronia. His plan was executed by Augustus. This basilica was 345ft long by 150ft wide (105 by 46m). It was open on three sides, with a double ambulatory portico and gallery surrounding its central hall, supported mostly on travertine stone piers rather than columns. The arcades of its two main façades were framed between half columns, like the Theatre of Marcellus. The courts of the Centumviri, the "hundred men", and the Chancery Court sat inside the grand building to judge suitably important cases. Augustus also rebuilt the Basilica Aemilia in 14BC after another fire, mainly on pre-existing lines. (It was damaged by yet another fire in 12BC.) It had a long narrow central hall about 295 by 90ft (90 by 27m) with an extra row of columns on its north-east side, which were probably decorative rather than structural. Indisputably decorative were the Doric columns supporting a luxuriant frieze on the side opening on to the Forum. The interior was paved with marble and lavishly decorated.

Trajan's Basilica Ulpia, which commemorated his family name and dominated his new Forum, was even larger and more luxurious, as befit a ruler who expanded Rome's frontiers to their

widest extent. Built across the Forum's north side, it measured about 560ft long by 200ft wide (170 by 60m). Its central nave, about 60ft (20m) wide, had two aisles on each side, divided off by giant columns of grey Egyptian granite. It probably had a flat beamed roof with galleries above the inner aisles that would have allowed a view of Trajan's column and a clerestory to provide light. It was dedicated along with his Forum in AD113. Despite its splendour and size, it is thought to have been relatively conservative in style.

Two centuries later, more radical elements in Roman architecture emerged in the huge Basilica Nova (New Basilica). Started by Maxentius, the last emperor actually to rule from Rome (AD306–12), it was finished by Constantine. In place of earlier columnar designs, its huge vaults copied those of the Baths of Caracalla and Diocletian. Also like them, its design concentrated on a very lavish interior at the expense of the plain exterior. Its central nave measured 260 by 80ft (80 by 25m), while its three cross-vaulted bays rose to a giddy 115ft (35m) from eight gigantic marble Corinthian columns. The concrete vaulted ceiling was decorated with painted sunken coffers. Constantine changed the axis of the building by

building another entrance with a staircase. In the apse he placed a gigantic seated marble and gilt statue of himself, staring out over his subjects. Even the surviving fragments – head and hands – still impress, as does all that remains of the basilica, the side vaults.

THE CURIA

Traditionally built by the Etruscan king Tullus Hostilius in the 6th century BC, the original Curia (Senate House) was the Curia Hostilia. Burnt down several times, it was replanned by Caesar in 44BC, completed by Augustus and henceforth called the Curia Julia. A tall gabled building, it was 69ft (21m) high by 88ft (27m) long and 59ft (18m) wide – the exact proportions recommended by Vitruvius – with three oblong windows above a shallow porch. A raised platform opposite the door inside seated the presiding magistrates, and senators sat facing each other on benches. From Augustus' time there were often 1,000 senators, more than the Curia could seat, so younger senators stood at the back. A statue of the winged goddess Victory, presented to the house by Augustus, probably stood by the dais. Diocletian restored the Curia after another fire in AD283.

Above: The Curia was burnt down again in 52BC and replanned by Julius Caesar in what became its final form.

Below: The arches of the Basilica Nova, started by Maxentius but finished and refurbished by Constantine, whose giant statue once dominated the interior.

TEMPLES: THE REPUBLIC AND THE EARLY PRINCIPATE

Above: The remains of the terrace of the temple of Claudius, completed under Vespasian long after his death.

Below: The Temple of Venus Genetrix, the mythical ancestress of the Julians, dominated Caesar's Forum.

As Roman temples evolved in later republican and early imperial Rome, they revealed the intermingling of native Italic traditions, derived ultimately from the Etruscans, with imported Greek styles. By the time of Augustus (30BC–AD14) something of a classical synthesis had been achieved. Although Roman architects continued to develop new ways of building temples, culminating in the Pantheon in the early 2nd century AD, this temple's novel form marked an effective end rather than a beginning to grand temple-building in Rome itself. In the provinces, however, especially in the east, new styles of temple building continued to emerge with often exuberant inventiveness.

The first large temple in Rome, and one that was always deeply revered, was that of Jupiter on the Capitoline Hill.

Traditionally started by the last monarch Tarquinius Superbus before 509BC, it was typically Etruscan in design. It stood on a podium made of tufa blocks about 13ft (4m) high and measured 203ft long by 174ft (62 by 53m), making it comparable in size to the biggest contemporary Greek temples. It had three *cellae* (inner chambers), with Jupiter in the central one flanked by his wife Juno and daughter Minerva. The temple's emphasis is very much on its front, where steps led to a portico of 18 columns, probably of stuccoed wood, with only three on the flanks and none at the rear. (Greek temples had columns all round.) Its overhanging roof was decorated with bright-painted terracotta ornaments and statues, some full-size. Etruscan statues, like the famous Apollo of Veii, could be remarkably fine.

GRAECO-ROMAN FUSION

The early Republic's temples, such as those of Saturn or Castor and Pollux, followed this Etruscan pattern in the 5th and 4th centuries BC, giving the city a colourful if scarcely classical air. However, by 200BC increasing contacts with the Hellenistic world had opened Roman eyes to far more sophisticated styles, while wealth from conquests enabled them to import Greek marble and craftsmen. The resulting temples show Greek detail based on a Roman plan.

The Greek architect Hermodorus built the first all-marble Temple of Jupiter Stator in 146BC. The slightly later Temple of Portunus, which is still almost intact, exemplifies the emerging Graeco-Roman synthesis: classically Greek Ionic columns rest on a raised Roman podium, the approach stairs and portico are at the front and the side pillar is engaged in the wall of the *cella* (inner chamber). This fusion is also apparent at the Temple of Hercules at Cori (*c.* 100BC). Here, the ground-plan

looks Italic, a style closely related to the Etruscans, but the fine Doric columns copy the current fashions of Hellenistic cities such as Pergamum.

Few temples were as wholly Greek in inspiration as the circular Temple of Hercules Victor (formerly called the Temple of Vesta) built soon after 100BC in the Forum Boarium. Made of Pentelic marble from Athens and probably the work of an Athenian architect (the names of most architects in Rome have not survived), its circular form is very Greek, as are the steps wholly surrounding it and the Corinthian capitals. Its construction marks the peak of the Hellenizing influence in Rome. A notable early exception (*c.* 150BC) to this Greek trend was the Temple of Fortuna Primigenia at Praeneste (Palestrina), whose dramatic use of vaulting and circular shapes anticipate the architectural revolution sometimes held to have started two centuries later with Nero's Domus Aurea (AD64–8).

AUGUSTUS' PROGRAMME
Augustus claimed in his autobiographical *Res Gestae* to have restored 82 temples in Rome in 28BC. Augustus' was certainly the biggest temple construction programme ever seen in Rome. His temples reveal his generally classical tastes.

Although generally not large – central Rome was now densely populated and space was at a premium – they were usually magnificently decorated. They were still set on tall podiums, often against a rear wall, with their columns grouped towards the front.

The emperor's grandest temple, that of Mars Ultor in his new Forum, was almost square, backed by a huge, slum-excluding firewall. Its giant Corinthian columns were set on a lofty podium of 17 steps which could only be approached from the front. Augustus' fine temple to his patron deity Apollo on the Palatine was built of solid Carrara marble between 36 and 28BC and adorned with famous Greek statues.

The century after Augustus' death in AD14 saw little development in temple-building, as attention was devoted chiefly to secular structures. In his 23-year-long reign, Tiberius did not even manage to complete the temple to the deified Augustus. Caligula finally finished it in the Ionic style. Nero started to build a temple to his deified stepfather Claudius, who had probably been poisoned by Agrippina, Nero's mother and Claudius' last wife. The emperor Vespasian, who admired Claudius, completed it in AD75. The enormous platform of the large structure still survives today.

Above: The Temple of Fortuna Primigenia at Praeneste (c.150BC) was a radically daring building in its use of vaults and circular shapes, anticipating much later styles.

Below: The Temple of Portunus typifies the Graeco-Roman fusion at its finest: classical Greek Ionic columns on an elevated Roman-style podium.

TEMPLES: THE PANTHEON AND AFTER

Above: The Pantheon's visionary union of portico and dome influenced many later buildings, such as the Church of St Mary in Mostal, Malta.

Often considered not just the most perfect Roman temple but the apogee of Roman architecture, the Pantheon, the temple to all the gods, was the emperor Hadrian's supreme architectural achievement in Rome. Its fame derives in part from its unusually well-preserved state (it was converted into the Church of Santa Maria ad Martyres in AD608) but it is indisputably merited as one of the most sublime of Roman buildings.

STRUCTURE OF THE PANTHEON
Two earlier temples had been built on the same site, one by Agrippa in 27BC and one by Domitian when Agrippa's temple burned down in AD80. Built between AD118–25, the Pantheon is composed of three rather disparate elements: a huge colonnaded porch, a tall middle block, and the rotunda that forms the temple's *cella* and supports its dome. The porch has 16 giant columns of the Composite order. These are made of grey and red Egyptian granite, with bases and capitals of white Carrara

Below: A partial cutaway of the dome of the Pantheon, revealing the coffering that lightened its weight. Its mathematically perfect proportions help explain its remarkable appeal.

or Greek marble. With an eagle on top of its pediment, the porch originally dominated a colonnaded piazza in front, looking higher than it does now (the surrounding ground has risen, as it has in most of Rome). The intermediary block, like the rotunda, was built of brick-faced concrete covered in marble. The rotunda's diameter and height are exactly the same, 142ft (43.2m), making it larger than any dome built in the next 1800 years. The dome springs 71ft (21.6m) above the floor. This means that a sphere of 142ft (43.2m) diameter would fit exactly inside the temple.

The rotunda rests on an immensely solid travertine and concrete ring 24ft (7.3m) wide and 15ft (4.5m) deep. It has eight load-bearing piers that form the building's framework, between which are curved or rectangular *exedrae* (recesses), each screened by two yellow Numidian marble columns, that may have once housed gods' statues. The piers support eight arches which run through the wall's core from inside out, part of a complex system of relieving arches that buttress the upper walls against the outward thrust of the dome.

The dome itself is built of concrete with an *oculus* (eye) opening 27ft (8.3m) at the top that gently illuminates the whole temple, drawing the eye up past the coffered roof to the sky, abode of the gods, far above. The upper parts of the dome are made of progressively lighter materials, with very light porous pumice stone being used at the top around the oculus. The 140 coffers of progressively diminishing size, arranged in five tiers of 28, also help to reduce the dome's weight while adorning its interior.

Like the roof tiles of the dome, these coffers were probably once gilded. Other interior decorations, surviving at least in part, are slabs of porphyry and dark green marble, while the floor was also paved

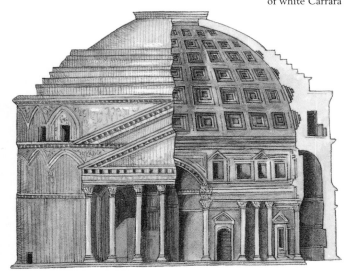

with marble. Only a small section of the original décor has been restored, but the Pantheon has retained more of its original decoration than any other Roman temple and the overall effect is still very lavish. The Pantheon impresses not only as a tremendous feat of engineering but also because it gives us a vivid idea of what a Roman temple may have been like. Its mathematically perfect proportions also elevate the spirit of visitors as they look up into the huge airy dome of this temple to all the gods.

EMPEROR AND ARCHITECT

Hadrian's other great temple, the Temple of Venus and Roma, stands on a high piece of ground between the Colosseum and Vespasian's Forum Pacis. It is also remarkable for a Roman temple for its very Greek design. Instead of standing on the usual Roman podium, it is set, like the Athenian Parthenon, in the centre of a rectangular platform on low steps that encircle it in Greek style. Hadrian was such a notorious philhellene that his enemies dubbed him *Graeculus* (Greekling).

Even more unusually, instead of having a single *cella*, the temple has two, back to back, both with apses, one for each goddess. (Roma Dea was the goddess of Rome itself.) These apses date from a rebuild under Maxentius. The original design had rectangular *cellae* back to back.

The temple was huge, 217ft wide by 348ft long (66 by 136m), with ten columns of grey Egyptian granite on its ends and 20 along its sides. Apollodorus, the brilliant architect of Trajan's great projects, who may also have been involved in designing the Pantheon, criticized the design, which was apparently Hadrian's own. Apollodorus claimed the temple was too wide for its height. Reputedly, the

Right: G.P. Panini's 18th-century painting of the Pantheon's interior, with its perfectly proportioned dome rising to an oculus *(central opening), makes it among the world's most magical buildings. It is also luckily the best preserved of Rome's temples.*

emperor had the architect exiled and then killed in AD129 for such impertinence, which suggests a prickly artistic pride in the emperor. The temple, dedicated in AD135, was rebuilt by Maxentius in the early 4th century AD. After Hadrian, Rome was no longer the one vital centre of great temple-building projects. Other cities across the empire competed with it increasingly and often showed more innovatory flair.

The Temple of Antoninus Pius and Faustina begun in AD141 in the Forum Romanum, which later became a church, was an unexciting rectangle. The Severans built temples to their favourite gods which were notable chiefly for their immense size and restored many older temples.

Before the days of Roman temple building drew to a close, the emperor Aurelian (AD270–5) built a temple to Sol Invictus (the Unconquered Sun), his favourite deity. This was apparently an unusual circular edifice within a large rectangular enclosure, that strongly suggests a Syrian influence.

Above: The Temple of Antoninus Pius and Faustina, Hadrian's successor, is a plain, even dull rectangular structure, preserved by being made into a church.

BUILDING THE THEATRES

Right: The theatre at Sabratha, Libya, is among the best-preserved of all Roman theatres. Its scaenae frons *(built-up backcloth) has been reconstructed with 96 marble columns on three storeys.*

Below: An actor wears a mask in a 3rd-century AD carving from the theatre at Sabratha, Libya. All actors in Greek and Roman theatres wore such masks.

The Greeks developed the world's very first permanent theatres; stone-built open-air structures where plays could be performed in front of huge audiences. However in their usual way, the Romans adapted the Hellenic model to make something distinctively Roman out of it. Whereas Greek theatres usually exploited natural sites to stunning advantage and retained a religious link with the god Dionysus, in whose worship dramas and comedies were originally staged, by the end of the Republic the Romans increasingly regarded theatre more as an entertainment than as a religious festival.

SUPPLY AND DEMAND

The Roman method of building massive structures raised on concrete vaults dispensed with the need for a suitable slope into which the hemicycle of a Greek theatre could be fitted. This meant Roman theatres could be built wherever there was a demand for them, principally in cities. Despite the huge success of early Roman comic playwrights such as Plautus (254–184BC) and Terence (195–159BC), Roman public taste tended increasingly to prefer mime or pantomime to plays proper. Changes in theatre design included making the theatre completely semicircular and turning the *orchestra* into seating for important officials rather than using it for performers. These changes can be seen clearly at the theatre of Taormina in Sicily. Here, the original Greek structure offered stunning views of Mount Etna behind until the Romans constructed a heavy *scaenae frons* (built-up backcloth). This obscured the view until its partial collapse!

Remarkably, there were no permanent theatres in Rome itself until very near the end of the Republic. Instead, temporary timber structures were built for each set of performances and then demolished.

(These temporary buildings could be grand, nonetheless. According to Pliny, Marcus Scaurus raised a structure in 58BC which, if timber-framed, was covered in glass and marble and could seat 80,000 people.) This lack was due mainly to the Senate's conservative puritanism, for it distrusted the loose morals that were then associated with the stage.

POMPEY'S THEATRE
It was only under the effective domination of the state by Pompey in the 50s BC that the first permanent stone theatre was built in Rome. It was completed in 55BC, just outside the old sacred *pomerium* (city boundary) in the flat Campus Martius. What Pompey built was not just a theatre, but a grand complex, with gardens and porticoes sheltering art galleries and other shops. As a sop to conservative sentiment, he described his theatre as a monumental stairway to the Temple of Venus Victrix (the Victory-bringer) sited at the top of the *cavea* (tiers of stepped seating). The theatre was made of concrete, which permitted the architects to support the seating on a series of radial and curving vaults, rather than having to seek a site on a hillside. Substantial parts of the substructures survive in cellars. Its *cavea* was 525ft (160m) in diameter and could seat about 27,000 spectators.

One of the oldest surviving theatres in Rome is that of Marcellus, which Augustus dedicated to the memory of his son-in-law in 13BC, fulfilling one of Caesar's grand projects. Still mostly extant, although partly converted into a hotel (it has also been a fortress and a palace in its time), it gives a good idea of an early Roman theatre. Built mainly of travertine stone with stone or concrete barrel-vaults, it closed the audience off from the hubbub of city life outside and so rendered the actors' dialogue audible on even the highest levels. There would have been retractable awnings against the sun to protect the spectators. The *scaenae frons* was as high as the *cavea* but seems to have been simple in design. The travertine façade had at least two series of ornamental arches framed by pillars, Doric on the ground floor and Ionic on the first. A third floor may have had Corinthian pillars or have been a simple attic floor. The theatre seated about 11,000 people.

THEATRES IN THE PROVINCES
To see further developments in Roman theatres we need to turn to other cities. At Lyons (Lugdunum), long the chief city of Gaul, a fine theatre was built under Hadrian (ruled AD117–38), enlarging and replacing an earlier building. Here pragmatic Roman architects showed that they were not averse to exploiting hillsides where they could. Next to this large theatre was a much smaller *odeum*, which was originally roofed and used for poetry recitals, lectures and musical performances. At Vienne, across the river Rhône, and even more notably at Orange in Provence, what became the standard type of theatre is still visible. Both theatres have a central *exedra* (recess) matched by two flanking ones in their monumental *scaenae frontes*. The full effect of a Roman theatre is best seen at Sabratha in modern Libya, where the *scaenae frons* has been reconstructed on all its three storeys with 96 marble columns.

Above: Arches flanked by columns from the Theatre of Marcellus. Dedicated by Augustus in 13BC and Rome's largest extant theatre, today part of it is a hotel.

Below: Masks epitomizing tragedy (left) and comedy (right). The Romans preferred the latter but also enjoyed violent melodramatic shows.

AMPHITHEATRES AND THE COLOSSEUM

No type of building is more closely associated today with the Roman empire than the amphitheatre. However, there was no permanent amphitheatre in Rome until the giant Flavian Amphitheatre, or Colosseum, was constructed. Built between AD70 and 80, its top storey may not have been completed until after the emperor Titus' sudden death in AD81.

THE GAMES AND PUBLIC ORDER

Rome's lack of amphitheatres was due less to the Senate's disapproval of gladiatorial activities *per se*, than to well-founded fears of public disorder and as riots had been known to occur after games in other cities. There had been full-scale riots at the Pompeii amphitheatre during games there in AD59, for example. (Pompeii has one of the empire's earliest and best-preserved arenas, dating from the 1st century BC.) Rome, however, was a much more heavily policed city.

Many games in the city took place not in amphitheatres but in the immense Circus Maximus, in theatres or even, in Rome's early days, in the Forum Romanum itself, when gladiatorial combat took place in the context of aristocratic funerals. Conversely, amphitheatres in the provinces such as Britain could seldom afford full gladiatorial fights, so amphitheatres were used instead for sporting contests or for military tattoos. Even so, the grand elliptical shape of amphitheatres, especially of the colossal archetype in Rome itself, remains justifiably linked with gladiatorial games.

A CROWD-PLEASING PROJECT

The emperors Gaius Caligula and Nero had loved gladiatorial games. These had been performed in temporary if lavishly decorated timber structures which were destroyed in the great fire of AD64. (A small stone amphitheatre built by Statilius Taurus, one of Augustus' generals, in 29BC was destroyed in the same fire.)

In a stroke of political genius, Vespasian decided to use the drained lake of Nero's Domus Aurea (Golden Palace) – which was detested less for its ostentation than for the huge area it ate up in the heart of Rome – for a great crowd-pleasing project: Rome's first, and the empire's greatest, permanent amphitheatre. Well-drained, with good clay subsoil for such a heavy building, in the very centre of the city, it was the perfect site. Work began early in Vespasian's reign (AD69–79) and Titus held typically splendid inauguratory games in AD80.

The Colosseum fully deserves its name, given by the historian Bede in the early Middle Ages either because of the colossal gold statue of Nero nearby, or because of its colossal size. A substantial part of the amphitheatre survives today. It was constantly pillaged for building materials over the centuries until Pope Benedict XIV pronounced it sanctified by the blood of martyrs in 1749, safeguarding the remainder. The Colosseum is still the most impressive extant building in Rome and a

Above: Detail of a model of the Colosseum, Rome's largest amphitheatre, built AD70–80, showing the statues that once adorned its arches.

Below: A view of the Colosseum as it appears today from the Via Sacra. Human depredations, not time, have ravaged the huge structure.

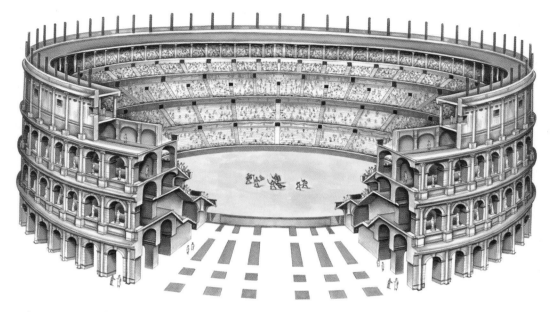

massive testament to the enduring skills of Roman engineers. Its typically elliptical outer shape measures 615 by 510ft (188 by 156m). The arena inside measures 282 by 177ft (86 by 54m) and its outer wall once rose to 171ft (52m), making it the tallest building in the city. It could accommodate an estimated 45–55,000 spectators.

To support the Colosseum's huge *cavea* (stepped seating), a vast ring of concrete 170ft (51m) wide and 40ft (12m) deep was laid. The lower part of about 20ft (6m) was cut into a trench while the upper, equal-sized part was contained inside a huge circle of brick-faced concrete above ground. These foundations supported a framework of loadbearing piers of travertine specially quarried near Tivoli. Between the piers ran radial walls of squared tufa up to the second floor. Almost all the vaults are barrel-vaults made of concrete, but some have brick ribs. About ten million cubic feet (100,000 cubic metres) of travertine were needed to build the façade alone and 300 tons of iron were used just for the nails. The façade has three tiers of low arches

framed respectively by Doric, Ionic and Corinthian columns, all semi-engaged (half columns) and purely decorative. The arches probably once had statues of gods or heroes in them, judging by depictions on coins. The top storey had tall Corinthian pilasters and originally had huge shields of gilded bronze, alternating with large windows, that would have gleamed impressively. Although this storey looks the most solid, it is in fact the lightest-built section.

The Romans erected this gigantic, complex structure with impressive speed, helped by their quasi-military organization of the process. Each material used in the building was handled by different groups of craftsmen, so that travertine could be added to the concrete core in one area while the final marble coatings were being laid in another. The whole structure was so massively built it withstood a lightning strike in AD217 – though it was closed for some years for repairs – and other assaults by recurrent earthquakes and the elements. Only human quarrying has done lasting damage.

Above: A cutaway section of the Colosseum in its prime, revealing the tiers of concrete barrel vaults and arches, suppported on load-bearing walls mostly of travertine stone buttressed by radial walls of tufa stone running between the piers.

Below: To Titus in AD80 fell the honour of inaugurating the amphitheatre that bears his dynasty's name, the Flavian Amphitheatre, with spectacularly lavish games.

Above: The amphitheatre at Arles in southern France is one of the finest extant outside Italy. Probably built in the late 1st century AD, its architect Crispus Reburrus also designed the amphitheatre at Nimes nearby.

Below: The emperor Vespasian (AD69–79), in whose reign the building of the immense Flavian Amphitheatre or Colosseum began.

SEATING BY RANK

The imperial box, richly decorated with coloured marbles, occupied the prime position on the short axis. Elsewhere, seating was allocated according to class or status. Augustus, as part of his attempted restoration of public morality, had tried to stipulate exactly who should sit where while watching performances in theatres, to reduce the opportunities for chatting up girls that Ovid so fondly described, and this seems to have applied in the Colosseum as well.

In the Colosseum, women were relegated to the topmost tiers – where they would have had the worst view but protection from the sun – except for the Vestal Virgins, whose high religious status overrode their lowly sexual status. They joined senators, equestrians (knights) and other dignitaries, often including ambassadors, in the smart seats in the lowest tier. Immediately above them was the first row for the general public, the *maenianum primum*, followed by the *maenianum secundum immum*, the *maenianum secundum summum* and finally the *maenianum secundum in ligneis*, with a gallery around that where ordinary spectators had to stand.

Some tickets were reserved in block-bookings for *collegia* (guilds) or for particular groups such as the citizens of Cadiz, privileges tenaciously preserved down the centuries. Tokens for all types of seats except the very best were given

out free for the games by the emperors on various occasions. This made admission to the games something of a lottery.

All seats were made of marble, another weight carried on the vaulted masonry substructure, except for the topmost tier, where they were made of wood to reduce the weight pressing down on the upper walls. No complete seats survive but fragments found in excavation have been pieced together to give an idea of what seating in the *maenianum secundum immum*, middling rank seats, were like. They were 17in (44cm) high by 21in (61cm) wide. Lower seats may have been more generous in size. Spectators reached their seats by climbing up or down rows of steps half the size of the seats. These led from the points where the inner stairs emerged into the *cavea* (stepped seating) from the myriad stairs and corridors below.

EXITS AND ENTRANCES

There were 76 public entrances, some of whose Roman numbers can still be seen. The emperor's monumental entrance, surmounted by a *quadriga* (four-horse chariot), was in the south, between entrances I (1) and LXXVI (76), a part of the amphitheatre that has been almost completely destroyed. Surviving far better is the next most important entrance, that of the consuls at the other end of the short axis. Renaissance drawings and remnants of stucco show that the vaulted entrance was originally richly decorated with stucco and other ornaments and probably topped by a pediment. The performers reached the arena directly by entrances at the long ends of the axis. The east entrance connected directly via a tunnel with the Ludus Magnus, the main imperial gladiatorial school nearby.

Ordinary spectators would have entered by their relevantly numbered arch and then climbed up stairs that connected the rings of circuit corridors, all of which were plastered and painted, until they reached their particular *vomitorium* (exit ramp) as the Romans punningly called the entrances. To protect the people from the 10ft (3m) drop from the seats into the stairwells, stone balustrades were provided. These were carved with animals such as dogs hunting deer or dolphins or mythological beasts such as sphinxes or griffins. Outside, barriers were erected around the travertine pavements that encircled the arena to control the eager crowds. Surviving stone posts suggest that chains were stretched between them.

ABOVE AND BELOW

The Roman audience was protected from the sun – and sudden rain showers – by a *velarium*, a huge canvas awning that covered the whole of the *cavea* and left only the arena open. Around the top of the amphitheatre are 240 stone brackets. These presumably once supported the rigging masts which held up this giant sunshade. (An alternative would have been long poles, as shown in a painting of Pompeii's amphitheatre, but the Colosseum may have been too vast for this simpler approach.) The whole system was operated by a special team of about 1,000 marines from the fleets at Misenum or Ravenna, who could also have acted as an auxiliary police force if needed. It has been tentatively calculated that the 240 ropes and the canvas would have weighed more than 24 tons.

Beneath the floor of the arena was an even more impressive network of subterranean passages and chambers which accommodated the wild beasts and the human performers before the games. About 246ft long by 144ft wide (75 by 44m) and 20ft (6m) deep, this seeming labyrinth was in fact organized with characteristic Roman efficiency, although later alterations and additions make the original structure hard to discern. It had five parallel corridors down the centre and three elliptical corridors along the sides. Beyond the outermost and narrowest corridor were 32 vaulted chambers which were used to cage the animals. Lifts operated by man-cranked windlasses lifted the animals up in their cages to trapdoors through which they sprang, bedazzled,

into the sunlit arena. The exact dimensions of their cages and the means by which the largest animals – elephants and hippopotami, for example – reached the arena remains under investigation. However, there were at least 30 lifts and many more trapdoors, so beneath the arena's floor a positive machine operated during the games.

The floor itself was probably of wood, although parts may have been made of stone slabs. It was covered with sand during the games to absorb the blood. The floor of the arena was probably not fully flooded to permit the large-scale *naumachiae* (re-enacted sea battles) historians describe and it is likely these took place elsewhere. However, early on there may have been a shallow pool for aquatic displays.

OTHER ARENAS

The Colosseum had few permanently built precursors but many imitators outside Rome, as an amphitheatre became an essential requirement for any self-respecting city. Most follow the same elliptical pattern and some have similar decorations on their exteriors, of arches flanked by columns. The amphitheatre at Verona, which held about 25,000 spectators, is *relatively* much larger than the Colosseum, as Verona was never one of the empire's biggest cities. The amphitheatres at Arles and Nîmes are particularly fine, as are many in Africa such as Thysdrus or Sabratha in Libya.

Above: The amphitheatre of Thysdrus (El Djem) in the fertile province of Africa (Tunisia) was built c. AD238. In its arena Gordian I was proclaimed emperor and later it became a refuge for the local inhabitants. It shows the still overwhelming influence of the Colosseum in Rome.

Below: Amphitheatres were relatively rare in most of the Eastern provinces, but theatres such as this at Pergamum in Asia Minor were sometimes adapted for combats or animal displays.

AQUEDUCTS AND SEWERS

Above: The Trevi Fountain in Rome is still supplied by the Acqua Vergine (Aqua Virgo), the only Roman aqueduct still functioning.

Below: These arches once carried the Aqua Claudia and the Aqua Anio Novus, the two aqueducts completed by Claudius in AD52.

The Romans were proud of their aqueducts and sewers, two essential aspects of civilization. As the geographer Strabo wrote early in the 1st century AD, "The Romans had foresight in matters about which the Greeks hardly cared, such as the construction of roads and aqueducts and of sewers that flush the filth of the city down to the Tiber... Water is brought to the city through aqueducts so copiously that positive rivers flow through the city and its sewers". At the end of the same century Frontinus declared, "Compare if you like the Pyramids or the useless if famous monuments of the Greeks with such a display of essential structures carrying so much water".

IMPERIAL CONFIDENCE

Sextus Julius Frontinus, who assumed the important post of *curator aquarum* (Water Commissioner) in AD96, wrote a book on Rome's water supply *De aquis urbis Romae* (On Rome's Aqueducts), that forms the basis of our knowledge. Classical Athens, among other cities, had piped fresh water to its citizens but Rome, the world's first giant city, needed water on an unprecedented scale, especially for its lavish *thermae* (imperial baths). Rome was also the first city to dig huge sewers to remove its waste waters. The aqueducts' giant arcades testify to something else: Roman confidence in its own power. Such highly visible and easily disrupted (or poisoned) water supplies were only feasible when no enemies closely threatened Rome. Ten major aqueducts built over six centuries finally supplied the city. The cutting of its aqueducts in AD537 during the Byzantine-Gothic wars symbolized the final end of ancient Rome.

PRACTICAL ENGINEERING

Rome's first aqueduct, the Aqua Appia, was built in 312BC by the censor Appius Claudius to supply water for the city's growing population. It had previously been supplied by springs or by the dubious water of the Tiber. Fed by springs near Albano, the aqueduct ran underground for 10 miles (16km); water was only carried above ground on arcades for about 100 yards inside the city. The Romans were far too practical to waste money building grandly arcaded aqueducts except when really needed.

Lead pipes were only used inside the city. For the most part, the aqueducts were stone-lined channels carrying water underground or just above it. As the Romans had no power to pump water uphill they had to ensure that the water always flowed downhill. The gradient of most aqueducts was surprisingly modest: about a 3ft drop per 1000, enough to keep the water flowing steadily.

Further aqueducts followed, at first slowly. The Anio Vetus in 272–269BC, which was almost four times as long as the Aqua Appia, took its water from the river Anio. The Aqua Marcia was started

in 144BC and paid for by booty from the sack of Corinth. It ran for 56 miles (91km) and was famed both for the purity of its waters and for the 6 miles (10km) of its length that ran on arcades, at some stages 95ft (29m) high.

The next two aqueducts were the Aqua Tepula started in 125BC and the Aqua Julia, with a capacity double that of the Tepula, built in 33BC. Both had similar lengths raised on arcades.

The Aqua Tepula was the work of Marcus Agrippa, Augustus' chief minister, who undertook a total restoration of all Rome's waterworks. In 19BC Agrippa also built the Aqua Virgo, the only aqueduct to enter the city from the north and the only one still functioning (as the Acqua Vergine, which supplies the Fontana di Trevi). Agrippa left his team of 240 slaves to Augustus. The latter made them public property and set up a permanent commission to oversee water supplies. The office of *procurator aquarum* was created by Claudius.

DEMAND FOR WATER INCREASES

Claudius built two aqueducts, the Aqua Claudia and the Aqua Anio Novus. Both had been started by the capricious emperor Caligula in AD38, partly to supply water for his *naumachiae* (re-enactments of sea-battles). Claudius completed them by AD52. The aqueducts' combined arcade marches for 6 miles (10km) across the Roman campagna before entering the city at what is now the Porta Maggiore.

The last great aqueduct, the Aqua Traiana, was built by Trajan in AD109. It brought good spring water from the hills north of Rome to the west bank (Trastevere), a region of the city that had been undersupplied. However, its elevation meant it could supply all the city's regions, which not every aqueduct could.

By this time the water supply to Rome had increased greatly. Since the building of the Aqua Claudia it had increased perhaps 15-fold to around 200 million gallons per day (900 million litres). This increase was

less a reflection of population growth than of the huge demands of the *thermae*. The aqueducts usually had settling tanks, to allow the sediment picked up en route to fall from the water. Water was also stored in *castella aquae* (reservoirs) or *stagna* (tanks) at the *thermae*.

GREAT SEWERS

Understandably, sewers were less widely lauded than aqueducts – Vitruvius discreetly ignores them. However, since the 6th century BC when the Cloaca Maxima (Great Drain) was dug as a drainage ditch, the Romans had built spacious, durable sewers made of well-crafted masonry.

Most Roman dwellings did not connect with the sewage system, however. This was chiefly because its reliance upon a constant, uninterrupted flow of water to flush it clear made it very expensive. Instead, many poorer Romans used chamber pots or the city's 144 recorded public latrines. Often lavishly decorated, these latrines provided facilities in which citizens could chat while seated in rows above the ever-flowing waters. Meanwhile, ever-flowing fountains flushed street litter into the drains. Down river from Rome, the Tiber cannot have been a salubrious stream.

Above: The Pont du Gard near Nimes in France forms the most famous part of all Roman aqueducts, partly because it has survived so well. Built by Agrippa between 20–16BC, this arched section rises 160ft (49m) above the river.

Below: The exit of the Cloaca Maxima (Great Drain), an unglamorous but vital aspect of public health. Started in the 6th century BC and restored by Agrippa, it bears testimony to the enduring skills of Roman engineers.

IMPERIAL BATHS

Above: In the 16th century Michelangelo created the vast Church of Santa Maria degli Angeli out of the frigidarium (cold bath), one section of the extant Baths of Diocletian.

Right: The frigidarium of the baths of Diocletian inspired the magnificent waiting room of Union Station, Washington DC. Designed by D.H. Burnham and completed in 1907, it has since been demolished.

The largest and architecturally most adventurous structures in Rome were the *thermae*, the imperial baths, of which 11 were finally built. By far the grandest and best-preserved are the four erected by the emperors Trajan (AD98–117), Caracalla (AD211–17), Diocletian (AD284–305) and Constantine (AD306–37).

BATHS AS A WAY OF LIFE

Roman *thermae* were far more than just baths. Their immense, lavishly decorated complexes – the largest enclosed spaces in the world before the 20th century – included libraries, gardens, art galleries, gymnasia, restaurants, meeting places and bordellos or rooms for sexual dalliance. For many Roman men, long, leisurely baths became a necessity, socially even more than hygienically, and occupied much of the afternoon. From the outset, the *thermae* used concrete vaulting for their construction. This material was ideally suited to such innovative and enormous buildings.

The first public baths appeared in the 2nd century BC. Pompeii had four large and many smaller public baths by the eruption in AD79. All showed the basic division into *frigidarium* (cold bath), *tepidarium* (warm) and *caldarium* (hot), the last heated by hypocausts, the piped hot-air floor and wall heating that became standard in baths throughout the empire.

The first full-scale Roman *thermae* were built by Agrippa in the Campus Martius, probably after 19BC, as they were supplied by the Aqua Virgo aqueduct which was completed that year. Little of Agrippa's original *thermae* remains – they were rebuilt in the 3rd century AD – but they probably had gardens and a gymnasium. For half a century they were the city's only *thermae*. Nero then built baths praised by the poet Martial: "What worse than Nero? What better than Nero's baths?" These were presumably more luxurious but they too were totally rebuilt between 222 and 227AD. Only with the *thermae* of the emperor Titus, inaugurated

in AD80, can we begin to glimpse imperial baths in their full splendour. Even here very little survives and we have to rely on the not necessarily accurate drawings made by the Renaissance architect Palladio. These suggest that the baths, built next to the Colosseum, were symmetrically planned with a terraced rectangular enclosure and the baths themselves placed on the north side, a layout broadly similar to the later, far better preserved baths of Trajan and Caracalla.

THE BATHS OF TRAJAN

Trajan was the most munificent of emperors and the one – after Augustus – with the most money (acquired in his Dacian conquests). He began Rome's first really grand *thermae* in AD104 after fire had damaged much of the Esquiline Wing of Nero's Domus Aurea (Golden Palace). Its wrecked upper floors were completely demolished, leaving only the vaulted ground floor, whose rooms and courtyards were joined together by vaulted roofs to raise the whole area to 154ft (47m) above sea level. The remainder of the hill was then levelled off to create a huge platform 1,115 by 1,083ft (340 by 330m). Almost certainly designed by Apollodorus of Damascus, Trajan's great architect, the *thermae* were three times as big as Titus' baths just south-west of them. They occupied 23 acres (9ha) and were able to accommodate many thousands of bathers at one time.

The *frigidarium* (cold bath), the tallest part of the building, was in the very centre of the baths. This was a large rectangular room with giant monolithic columns of red and grey granite placed in its corners. These seemed to carry the building's soaring roof but were in fact wholly decorative, as the piers behind them really supported the cross-vaulted ceiling. Like the rest of the interior of the baths, the *frigidarium* would have been richly decorated and probably coffered. There were four cold plunge pools. On either side were large colonnaded areas open to the sky and closed off by big

half-domed *exedrae* (recesses) called *palaestrae*, where bathers would exercise before entering the hot rooms. A fraternity of athletes was based there for approximately two centuries.

To the north-east of the baths lay the big *natatio* (swimming pool), open to the sky and flanked by a colonnade. On the other side of the *frigidarium* lay the small *tepidarium* (warm bath), which was maintained at an intermediate temperature to acclimatize bathers to the heat to come.

On the south-west front of the building, carefully sited to capture the heat of the afternoon sun, was the *caldarium*, the (very) hot bath. Its curved bay windows were possibly double-glazed, an example of solar heating. Glass had become more widely available by this time but the row of tall windows along the south side was still startlingly innovatory. The *caldarium* had apses on three sides, each containing a hot plunge pool. The whole vast room, and the similar but smaller hot chambers adjacent, was heated by hypocausts not only in the floor – which might have been almost uncomfortably hot to walk on – but also in the walls and even the ceilings. The heat for both the hypocausts and the hot water came from a series of *praefurniae* (furnaces) beneath, stoked by slaves

Above: One of the great hemicycles of the Baths of Trajan on the Esquiline Hill in Rome, on the north-east side of the baths. Completed in AD109, they surpassed all preceding baths in their grandeur and lavishness.

Below: Mosaic floor decorations such as this were common in the imperial baths.

1,000 years later sometimes corroborate and sometimes contradict the Marble Plan.) To the enclosure's north-west and north-east ends were other *exedrae*. Each contained a *nymphaeum* (ornamental fountain). The open spaces between the baths and the perimeter buildings were planted out as gardens. The whole complex was made of brick-faced concrete, covered in plain stucco on the outside but lavishly decorated in coloured marble with pillars, pilasters and marble floors throughout the interior.

Water for the baths was supplied partly by Trajan's new aqueduct, the Aqua Traiana, carried in pipes over bridges from its debauchment on the west bank, and partly from the neighbouring reservoir known as the Sette Salle, a two-storeyed building with a capacity of about 1½ million gallons (7 million litres). This was probably supplied by the Aqua Claudia, rather than the Aqua Traiana. The whole complex was inaugurated in AD109 and immediately eclipsed all its predecessors in grandeur and luxury.

THE BATHS OF CARACALLA
Although Rome's population probably did not grow appreciably in the century after Trajan built his *thermae* – in fact, it probably shrank after the great plague of AD164–5 – its citizens' expectations continued to increase, despite mounting problems on the empire's frontiers. To meet these expectations and to boost his own rather shaky popularity, the emperor Caracalla (ruled AD211–17) decided to build a grand new complex of baths to the south of the Forum Romanum.

In the century since Trajan's rule, architecture in Rome itself had not progressed much but in the provinces it had. Caracalla's dynasty, the Severans, came from Africa. This perhaps partly explains the daring size and shape of his *thermae*, dedicated in AD216 and among the most impressive ruins in Rome. Although they follow the general pattern of Trajan's baths, the central block is detached from its surrounding enclosure. This is nearly

Above: A fanciful recreation of the Baths of Caracalla by the Victorian painter Lawrence Alma-Tadema captures the atmosphere of luxury, even licentiousness, often associated with the great imperial baths that was much attacked by the early Christians.

who worked in abominably smoke-filled confinement out of sight of the bathers who sweated so contentedly in their magnificent marble halls.

The buildings around the perimeter included two hexagonal half-domed *exedrae*, about 95ft (29m) in diameter, on the south-west and south-east corners. These were probably Latin and Greek libraries respectively, for the Romans tried to cater for the mind as well as the body. Their brick-faced concrete skeletons survive, although most of Trajan's *thermae* have not. (We rely for information about the baths on two written records, the *Forma Urbis Romae* (the Marble Map of Rome) from the Severan period and the unknown medieval architect called the Anonymous Destailler, whose works

500yds (460m) square and encloses an area of almost 50 acres (20ha). Here water could be stored and the subsidiary amenities now expected of a great *thermae* be provided. The main bath block itself was a simple rectangle 712ft long by 360ft wide (214 by 110m), except for the massive semicircular projecting *caldarium* (hot bath). Its huge circular, elliptical or oblong rooms open logically into each other along two axes that intersect at the great three-bay *frigidarium* in the centre. Its three cross-vaults rose above the level of the adjacent rooms, lighting it by eight lunettes (semicircular openings). Connecting but insulating the *caldarium* and *frigidarium* was the *tepidarium*, a room whose markedly small doors prevented heat entering or escaping from it.

While only four doorways pierced the complex's blank north-east front, the south-west front had a long line of great windows to absorb the sun's rays into the series of hot rooms. Dominating these was the huge circular *caldarium*, a domed hall whose span of 115ft (35m) approached that of the dome of the Pantheon and whose height exceeded it. Beneath each of the eight huge windows that bravely pierced the dome's drum – a feat that no earlier Roman architect had attempted because of the structural problems – was a hot plunge bath.

On the north side of the building was the *natatio* (swimming pool), shielded from the north by a high wall and protected from the sun's rays by the bulk of the *frigidarium*. At either end of the long axis was a *palaestra* (exercise yard) surrounded by terraced porticos. Built of the now standard brick-faced concrete and presenting a blank face to the outer world except on its many-windowed south–western front, the Baths of Caracalla were decorated on the inside with unprecedented lavishness, with multi-coloured marbles and mosaics and a profusion of ornaments. Roman taste may have abandoned the restraint of Augustan classicism but the subtle contrast of differently shaped rooms, the alternation

of light and shadow as bathers moved into and out of the sunlight, above all the soaring height of the vaults above, demonstrated a new technical mastery.

THE LAST *THERMAE*

The political chaos of the mid-3rd century precluded much further lavish building apart from the Baths of Decius on the Aventine and the Palace of the Gordians on the Via Praenestina. However, although Rome was no longer the only capital city of the empire, it retained its imperial mystique. Once Diocletian (ruled AD284–305) had restored order and instituted the new Tetrarchy (four-ruler system), he decided to build another massive set of baths as part of his overall renovation of Rome. In AD298 he began building his *thermae*, broadly following Caracalla's design but with greater simplicity and less daring. It was even larger, its central block being 785ft long by 475ft wide (240 by 144m). Its central axis from east to west allowed a view right through the resulting alternation of light and shadow. Again, the *caldarium* was a curved room on the south-west side, with other elliptical or polygonal rooms, but the overall effect was less dramatic. The exterior was rather stark, the interior imperially magnificent.

Constantine I, the last emperor to build significantly in Rome, erected his own *thermae* closer to Rome's centre. Against the rather severely rectilinear plan of Diocletian's baths, this made great use of curves, circles and semicircles, at least according to the drawings made by Palladio in the 16th century. However, it probably still followed the essentially symmetrical pattern pioneered by the Baths of Titus over 200 years before. The imperial *thermae* were prodigious users of fuel as well as water and could not long survive the general collapse of the Western empire in the 5th century. Early Christians generally disapproved of over-lavish baths, with all their sensual connotations, and they were abandoned in the West. In Byzantium, however, *thermae* survived.

Above: Parts of the massive, brick-faced concrete walls of the Baths of Caracalla still stand, but the internal splendour of the building has long since vanished.

Below: The Thermal Baths, as the Antonine Baths in Carthage are known (built AD146–62), which rivalled those of Caracalla in size.

CIRCUSES

Chariot-racing was immensely popular with Romans from a very early date. By 500BC, races were being held in the Circus Maximus (biggest or grandest circus). This was located in an area in the valley between the Palatine and Aventine Hills connected with the gods that the races originally honoured.

ORIGINS OF THE CIRCUS MAXIMUS

For a long time the Circus Maximus was only a track with temporary wooden stands and a simple central barrier round which chariots raced. Rulers from Julius Caesar onwards added or made improvements to create an increasingly grand, permanent structure and it was entirely redeveloped by the emperor Trajan. Other circuses were smaller and used mainly for ceremonial displays.

In the late 4th century BC, the first wooden *carceres* (starting gates) were built at one end of the Circus Maximus. In 196BC, Lucius Stertinius erected an arch with gilded statues at the entrance. The central eggs for timing races are recorded as having been restored in 179BC, so they must predate this. Real developments started with Julius Caesar (49–44BC). He built the first tier of stone seating with a ditch 10ft (3m) wide in front to protect spectators from wild beasts, for *venationes* (wild beast displays) also took place there.

Augustus created the *pulvinar*, the imperial box, from which emperors could majestically look down on the races. It later connected directly with the grand Domus Flavia (Imperial Palace), completed by Domitian in AD92. Augustus transformed the *spina* (central barrier) by adding a 13th-century BC obelisk brought from Heliopolis, centre of the Egyptian sun-cult. Augustus' general Agrippa added bronze dolphins as a second lap counter device. Claudius built monumental stone gates but the rest of the Circus, still built of timber, burnt down in the great fire of AD64. Titus added a triumphal entrance arch to celebrate his sack of Jerusalem. Finally, Trajan transformed the structure into a massive monument. Built mostly of brick-faced concrete covered in marble, stone or stucco, the Circus could now seat an estimated 300,000 people, about a quarter of the city's population, making it the largest single structure for public entertainment in the world. (Ancient sources give even higher figures for spectators.)

In Diocletian's reign (AD284–305) the top part of the seating collapsed killing 13,000 spectators. Constantius II erected Rome's tallest obelisk at 112ft (32.5m) in it on his visit in AD357. The site remains but only fragments of the building survive, including the curved end, for it has been plundered for building materials.

Above: A 4th-century AD relief showing the races in full frenzy in the Circus Maximus conveys the heady mixture of glamour and danger that so captivated the Roman populace.

Below: A Roman charioteer on a quadriga *(four-horse chariot), a dangerous yet common form of racing chariot, with the outer horses attached to the chariot only by loose reins.*

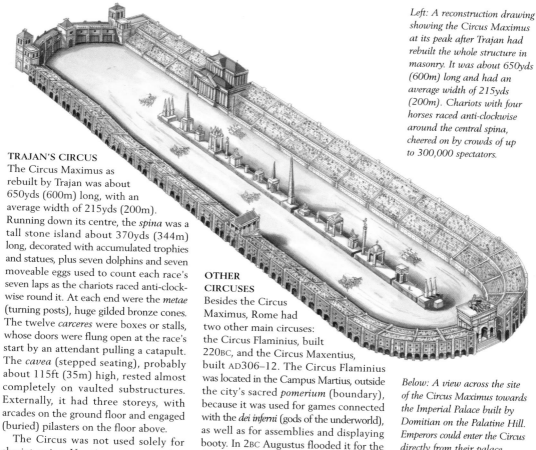

TRAJAN'S CIRCUS

The Circus Maximus as rebuilt by Trajan was about 650yds (600m) long, with an average width of 215yds (200m). Running down its centre, the *spina* was a tall stone island about 370yds (344m) long, decorated with accumulated trophies and statues, plus seven dolphins and seven moveable eggs used to count each race's seven laps as the chariots raced anti-clockwise round it. At each end were the *metae* (turning posts), huge gilded bronze cones. The twelve *carceres* were boxes or stalls, whose doors were flung open at the race's start by an attendant pulling a catapult. The *cavea* (stepped seating), probably about 115ft (35m) high, rested almost completely on vaulted substructures. Externally, it had three storeys, with arcades on the ground floor and engaged (buried) pilasters on the floor above.

The Circus was not used solely for chariot racing. *Venationes* were staged in it – far more people could see wild beast shows there than in the Colosseum – and especially odious criminals, including early Christians, suffered the horrendous fate of *damnatio ad bestias* there: they were tied to a stake and savaged to death by goaded carnivores. In AD204, the emperor Septimius Severus staged special games in which a massive, specially built ship fell apart in a mock *naufragium* (shipwreck) to disgorge 700 wild animals, who then fought each other. At other less sanguinary times, the huge arena filled with stall-holders, fortune-tellers and buskers who turned it into a lively market.

OTHER CIRCUSES

Besides the Circus Maximus, Rome had two other main circuses: the Circus Flaminius, built 220BC, and the Circus Maxentius, built AD306–12. The Circus Flaminius was located in the Campus Martius, outside the city's sacred *pomerium* (boundary), because it was used for games connected with the *dei inferni* (gods of the underworld), as well as for assemblies and displaying booty. In 2BC Augustus flooded it for the display and slaughter of 36 crocodiles, so it clearly had a retaining wall, but it was never monumentalized into a stone structure and was later overshadowed by the Theatres of Pompey and Balbus nearby.

The Circus Maxentius, built outside the city on the Via Appia as part of Maxentius' complex of villa and mausoleum, is large – about 570 by 100 yds (520 x 92m) – but having a low *cavea*, it could accommodate only 15,000 spectators, members of Maxentius' court and hangers-on. It shows interesting architectural developments. The *spina*, for example, is placed off-axis to allow for the crowding of chariots at the start.

Below: A view across the site of the Circus Maximus towards the Imperial Palace built by Domitian on the Palatine Hill. Emperors could enter the Circus directly from their palace.

TRIUMPHAL ARCHES

Above: One of the first triple triumphal arches, the Arch of Tiberius was built in Orange, France to commemorate the defeat of the rebel Julius Sacrovir in AD21. Its large central arch is flanked by Corinthian columns and smaller side arches.

Few monuments are more characteristically Roman than the freestanding monumental triumphal arches that they built, usually to celebrate military or political triumphs. Although the Romans did not invent the arch, they were the first to use it to commemorate such events ceremonially. Cities around the empire and, after the Renaissance, across the world, also built triumphal arches, showing how deeply this monument has caught the Western imagination.

COMMEMORATING VICTORY
In its essence a triumphal arch is a vaulted passageway apparently, but not in reality, supported on pilasters with a decorated frieze (sculpted entablature) and an attic carrying statues, trophies and, in ancient Rome, inscriptions.

The first *fornices*, honorific arches with statues, were built in Rome in the 2nd century BC by nobles commemorating their exploits. These include those of Lucius Stertinius in the Circus Maximus and in the Forum Boarium in 196BC and of Scipio Africanus on the road up to the

Capitoline in 190BC. No arches of the Republican period remain, chiefly because Augustus so radically reordered the Forum that few monuments unconnected with his family or faction survived.

Augustus built his Actian Arch, commemorating victory over Mark Antony, next to the temple of his adopted father, the deified Julius Caesar, in 29BC. After his Parthian "victory" of 19BC – actually just a notably successful diplomatic settlement – he either rebuilt it more grandly or built a new arch on the other side of the temple.

In its final form it was, unusually, a triple gateway, the central grand arch flanked by two smaller, attached openings that were not arched but simple flat, pedimented gateways. Above the central arch was a statue of Augustus in a *quadriga* (four-horse chariot). On the sides of the arch, marble inscriptions listed the names of *triumphatores* (generals granted triumphs) from the time of Romulus, Rome's mythical founder, thus linking Augustus with his predecessors. Augustus also built a smaller arch to Gaius and

Right: The last great arch in Rome was the triple arch of Constantine built AD315. It looks back to earlier arches, most notably in its plundering of older material. These panels show Marcus Aurelius' head awkwardly reworked to resemble Constantine.

Lucius, his grandsons and intended heirs who both died young. This was probably located on the temple's other side. Arches were built around the Forum for some later victorious generals, all of them descendants of Augustus, such as that of Germanicus in AD16 and of the younger Drusus in AD19. A half-ruined arch to Germanicus survives at Pompeii.

Perhaps the finest arch to survive extant in Rome is that of Titus (ruled AD79–81), the Flavian emperor who was so generous to the Roman people and so merciless to his enemies. Built at the top of the Via Sacra (Sacred Way), it was finished after his death by his brother Domitian. Fine white Pentelic marble from Greece covered its concrete core (it was restored in 1821), but it impresses chiefly through the calm dignity of its lines. Slightly taller than it is wide, its single opening is flanked by massive piers with eight half columns of the Composite order – a favourite in Flavian architecture – standing on a high podium and supporting an architrave and frieze. This depicts Titus' triumphal procession in Rome after sacking the temple in Jerusalem. The eloquent simplicity of the arch marks a peak of Roman classicism. The fine arch to Trajan at Benevento in southern Italy is so similar in design that it could be by the same architect.

The next great arch extant is that of Septimius Severus built in AD203 right over the Via Sacra. A grand triple monument, it is 68ft high by 76ft wide (21m by 23m). It was originally surmounted by a *quadriga* bearing the emperor and his two sons Caracalla and Geta. Besides its size, it is notable for the four great panels depicting Severus' victorious eastern campaign, in which he had won the new province of (northern) Mesopotamia. Rejecting the classical three-dimensional realism that had so long been the rule, the flattened style of its carvings anticipates that of the later empire. By contrast, an austere yet classically proportioned arch erected by Gallienus (ruled AD253–68) survives but is squashed between later buildings on the Esquiline Hill.

THE LAST ARCH
Constantine I was the last of the arch-building emperors in Rome whose work survives. His triple arch, completed in AD315, celebrates his victory over Maxentius. Although it is the biggest in Rome and generally imitates Severus' closely in design, it is hardly the most elegant. Longer than it is wide, it looks rather earth-bound compared to earlier arches. Its finest carvings were lifted from other monuments – of the Flavian, Trajanic and Antonine periods – while the original carvings are poorly modelled. The tradition of carving sculptural reliefs in stone had almost died out in Rome 50 years earlier. Tastes were changing anyway. Newer buildings, such as the Basilica Nova and the Baths of Diocletian relied on coloured marble, stucco and mosaic to embellish their interiors, leaving the exterior relatively austere. Constantine's arch was in fact antiquarian, looking back to an age that had already ended.

Above: The noble dignity of the Arch of Trajan at Benevento, dedicated in AD114, stems from its fine proportions and its Parian marble covering.

Below: The Arc de Triomphe, Paris, is the largest modern arch emulating Rome's arches.

TRIUMPHAL COLUMNS

Commemorative or triumphal columns celebrated great individuals, especially military men. The Romans, like the Greeks or Egyptians, were passionate about perpetuating their fame by the most durable means available, but the idea of erecting marble columns topped by bronze or marble statues seems to have been a wholly Roman one. The practice was revived in the Renaissance and has long continued: one of London's most famous landmarks is Nelson's Column, which dominates Trafalgar Square.

Columns known as *columnae rostratae* were erected from the 3rd century BC. One of the earliest is the Column of Gaius Duilius, a column with ships' prows dating from 260BC. By the 2nd century BC, relatively small columns celebrating successful Republican nobles' exploits were being erected in and around the Forum Romanum. (An ancient pillar, the Maenian Column, originally stood near the old prison to the west of the Curia Hostilia, the first Senate House, but it was a landmark helping officials tell the time of day, not a memorial.) The Forum, however, soon became so cluttered with monuments of various sorts, including statues, arches and columns, that in 158BC the censors ordered that space be cleared to let citizens move around easily.

TRAJAN'S COLUMN

The truly great triumphal columns of Rome were built not in the still half-Republican Forum Romanum but in the grand new complexes of the emperors. Trajan, perhaps the most grandiose of Rome's imperial builders, crowned his resplendent new basilica with a triumphal column rising just beyond its tall roof. This

Left: Trajan's great column soars 131ft (40m) into the sky, the grandest in Rome. In front are the columns of the Basilica Ulpia.

Above: A river god, personifying the River Danube, looks up at the Roman soldiers triumphantly crossing the Danube during Trajan's Dacian campaign.

became the unsurpassed archetype of such monuments. Built in AD112–13, probably by Trajan's famous architect Apollodorus of Damascus, it is truly prodigious. The column is 125ft (38m) high including its base and composed of 19 giant drums of Carrara marble, each weighing about 40 tons. It is both classical, comprising a single gigantic Doric column in form, and radical in its design, with a hollow interior up which a spiral staircase of 185 steps winds to a balcony.

The column is also remarkable for its carvings. These form a continuous frieze which coils around the column like a gigantic illustrated marble scroll about 600ft (180m) long. The carvings depict in amazingly graphic detail the story of Trajan's recent conquest of Dacia (Romania) and give us an impression of the Roman army in its conquering prime.

Scenes of the emperor addressing his troops, of legionaries crossing rivers, marching, building and fighting, and of the wounded being tended, are punctuated halfway up by a figure of the goddess Victory. She is flanked by trophies that form a link with the sculptures at the column's base which show captured barbarian equipment. The columns' higher parts would have been more visible than they are today, as the upper storeys of the adjacent libraries and basilica would have allowed people to view them halfway up. The frieze is one of the finest examples of Roman low relief. Brimming with artistic energy, it had a great influence on carvings around the empire in the following century.

Within this colossal monument to self-glorification was a tomb-chamber for Trajan himself. This was almost certainly not part of the original plan in view of the spiral staircase within the column. Trajan's ashes were laid there after he had died in Tarsus in Asia Minor in AD117 on his way home from his disastrous Parthian war.

The column owes its unusually good state of preservation to Pope Gregory the Great (ruled AD590–604). Reputedly, Gregory was so moved by a relief showing Trajan helping a grieving woman that he prayed to God to release the emperor's soul from hell. According to the story, God agreed, Trajan became the only pagan ruler thus spared and the land around his column was declared sacred.

The gilded bronze statue of the emperor that once topped the column was replaced in 1587 by a statue of St Peter. Restored for Rome's millennial jubilee in 2000, it now gleams with almost pristine freshness.

IMITATING TRAJAN

Trajan's superb column was hard to match but Marcus Aurelius (ruled AD161–80), who fought even longer if less victorious wars on the Danube, had a column erected to him after his death by Commodus, his son. About 100ft (30m) high, it is composed of 28 drums of

marble. It also has an internal staircase and a spiral relief depicting Marcus' wars. The relief's overall tone, however, is very different. In place of Trajanic triumphalism, there is a sense of exhaustion and despair and it is carved in a manner which indicates that the tradition of classical realism was approaching its end. The tradition of self-glorification did not die so easily, however. In Constantinople, the emperors Theodosius I (AD378–95) and Arcadius (AD395–408) both raised similar columns to themselves, of which little survives.

One of the strangest uses for such columns in the now Christian empire was as ostentatiously uncomfortable retreats for saints or hermits, who clambered up, dislodged the pagan statue on top and then squatted between heaven and earth, to be admired by the faithful below. St Simeon Stylites, the Syrian saint (AD387–459) was only the first of many such holy exhibitionists.

Above: The Roman obsession with perpetuating their fame posthumously depended partly on a literate posterity that could read such fine inscriptions as this one, which was dedicated to the deified emperor Titus.

Below: The figures on Marcus Aurelius' column (c. AD180) seem dumpy and exhausted by their years of bitter war on the Danube.

CHURCHES

Above: The Basilica of Sant' Apollinare in Classe, near Ravenna, was begun in AD490 and finished under the Byzantines.

Below: The simple rectangular form of the Basilica of Old St Peter's, Rome, begun c. AD333.

Poverty, persecution and expectations of the imminent end of the world meant the first Christians built little. However, when Constantine became the first Christian emperor after AD313, he inaugurated a vigorous programme of church building that continued throughout the vicissitudes of the next two centuries.

A NEW ARCHITECTURE
Christian worship differed radically from pagan cults. In the latter, the image of the god was often secluded in a small, mysteriously dark shrine inside a temple's *cella* (inner chamber) and only taken out on special festivals, with most worshippers remaining in the outer court. Some old temples did become churches, as the Pantheon did in AD608, but its shape and size were both exceptional. Christian worship required the presence of the whole body of the faithful for prayers,

responses and sermons and much larger, more open buildings were needed. Architects turned to the great basilicas that now dominated many cities across the empire for inspiration. Trajan's grand but architecturally simple basilica, with its colonnaded aisles, high beamed roof and apses at each end well suited for altars, with lighting provided by clerestories above, provided a model for many churches in the 4th and 5th centuries AD.

BUILDING THE BASILICAS
Across the River Tiber on the Campus Vaticanus, the site of St Peter's martyrdom in AD64 in the Circus of Nero, Constantine donated land to Pope Sylvester I to build Old St Peter's, the foremost church in Western Christendom. Started in AD333 (the present domed church dates only from the 16th century), it was a simple rectangular building with a flat, timber-beamed ceiling supported by colonnaded naves. The basilica had a broad lateral transept placed, exceptionally, between the apse and the nave to allow the circulation of pilgrims who came to venerate St Peter's tomb. Above the tomb, a marble *baldachino* (canopy) with spiral fluted columns was erected. The basilica's colonnaded nave and aisles were used both as the prototypical covered cemetery – many saints and popes are buried there, but there had never been burials within pagan temples – and as a banqueting and funeral hall. Outside, a central fountain was provided for religious ablutions, the only type of washing that ascetic early Christians admired. The whole complex was completed by AD344.

In Rome proper, a grand example of early basilicas was the Basilica Constantinia on the Lateran Hill. This is known today as San Giovanni in Laterano

(St John's in the Lateran). Begun by Constantine in AD313, he gave the basilica and its adjacent land to the pope. Until 1309, when the papacy left Rome for its exile in Avignon, the adjoining Lateran palace was the official papal residence.

Today's basilica retains the original groundplan but has been destroyed by fire twice and rebuilt many times, most notably by Borromini in 1646. The Constantinian church, built of brick-faced concrete, was reputedly very splendid, with seven gold altars, 100 chandeliers and 60 gold candlesticks to illuminate its mosaics. Contrasting with this imperial grandeur is the church of Santa Costanza, built as a mausoleum for Constantine's canonized daughter Constantia in AD340. Its dome is supported by a circular arcade resting on 12 pairs of fine columns, while its barrel-vaulted ceiling has marvellous extant mosaics showing flora and fauna and the grape harvest.

Church-building continued, if more slowly, after Constantine's move east. San Paolo fuori le Mura (St Paul's Outside the Walls), begun in AD385, has columns supported by arches while a giant arch divides its nave from the apse. Unfortunately, the church was drably restored after a fire in 1823. Surviving much better is Santa Maria Maggiore (Great St Mary's). It originated in a dream Pope Liberius had in AD356 in which the Virgin Mary told him to found a church on the spot where snow fell in August. It was actually built under Pope Sixtus III (AD432–40). Its imposing, classical giant Ionic columns line the colonnaded nave. Santa Sabina on the Aventine is another elegant, well-preserved example of this short-lived but remarkable classical revival.

BYZANTINE ARCHITECTURE

Late Roman styles developed into Byzantine mainly outside Rome. At Ravenna, which was the capital of the Western empire from AD402, then of Ostrogothic kings and finally of Byzantine *exarchs* (governors), the empress Galla Placidia constructed a mausoleum for

herself and her brother Honorius in AD425. Its mosaics reveal a joyfully pastoral vision of Christianity. Grander but heavier are the mosaics in the Basilica of Sant'Apollinare in Classe outside Ravenna. Begun in AD490 under the Ostrogoths and finished in AD549 by the Byzantines, it is still a basilica-type church, as most churches in the West were always to be.

However, in the East a new architecture was emerging in the radical designs of the cathedral of Hagia Sophia in Constantinople, built under the emperor Justinian I (ruled AD527–65). A centrally planned church whose 180ft (55m) dome seems to float without visible support – "Marvellous in its grace but terrifying because of its seemingly insecure composition", as the writer Procopius put it – it satisfied Byzantine needs for a cruciform church and must have later inspired Islamic builders. However, its construction marks an effective end to the period of truly Roman architecture.

Above: The mausoleum of Galla Placidia in Ravenna, one of the finest buildings of the 5th century AD in Ravenna, was renowned for its mosaics.

Below: The high point of Byzantine architecture is the cathedral of Hagia Sophia. Its simple, seemingly unsupported dome was hugely influential.

IMPERIAL PALACES

The English word palace comes from Latin, from *palatium*, the hill that gave its name to the imperial residence on the Palatine Hill. This majestic complex of courtyards, halls, basilica, stadium and private apartments, built by Domitian (AD 81–96), became the palace of all subsequent emperors, some of whom enlarged it. The official wing was called the *Domus Flavia* (Flavian Palace) and its private section was the *Domus Augustana* (Palace of Augustus), so the whole building became known as the *palatium* and the word passed into almost all West European languages (*palais, palacio, palazzo, palast*).

The house on the Palatine overlooking the Circus Maximus was not the first great imperial residence, for Nero's Domus Aurea (Golden Palace) had anticipated and in some ways exceeded it in extent and grandeur. Nor was it to be the last word in Roman palace architecture. As the tetrarchs and other rulers of the later empire set up their own administrative capitals – at Trier, Milan, Arles, Thessalonica, Nicomedia and finally Constantinople – they built palaces to match their grand pretensions, complete with baths and circuses. Most remarkable of all was Diocletian's massive retirement home to which he retreated in AD 306: a palace-fortress at Split on the Dalmatian coast. The building of these imperial palaces both incorporated and accelerated some of Rome's greatest achievements in architecture, especially the use of vaults and domes.

Left: The ruins of the imperial palace complex built on the Palatine Hill, as seen from the Circus Maximus.

Above: An aureus *(gold coin) of Augustus, first and most successful of emperors, whose own house was deliberately modest and unregal in its size and appearance.*

Below: The infant Hercules killing snakes. A fresco from the House of the Vettii at Pompeii, typical of the sort of decorations the earlier imperial palaces would have had.

THE PALACES OF AUGUSTUS AND HIS HEIRS

Augustus, the first and most revered Roman emperor, lived in an almost ostentatiously modest house, not in a palace. On his return to Rome in 29BC after defeating Antony and Cleopatra, Octavian (as he was called until 27BC) did not build himself anything remotely regal.

A HOUSE FOR THE *PRINCEPS*

Republican Rome had never had proper palaces, although Octavian had seen, indeed probably slept in, the palaces of Hellenistic monarchs such as the Ptolemies in Egypt. However, this was not the image he wanted to project in Rome, a city still proud of its Republican traditions. Instead, in line with his attempts to appear only as the *princeps*, the first among (almost) equals of the Roman nobility, he chose to live in the house that had once belonged to the orator Hortensius, a rival of Cicero.

This was a dignified, good-sized but not exceptional *domus* (detached house) on the Palatine Hill, a favoured location for wealthy nobles.

Some nobles in the Republic's later decades had built themselves very large and luxurious houses, on the Palatine among other hilly – and healthier – areas, but usually near the Forum, the heart of Roman life. The house of Aemilus Scaurus on the Palatine, for example, was sold in 53BC for 14,800,000 sesterces, an immense sum. Augustus' house probably still had an old-fashioned atrium, centred on its *compluvium* (pool). This was traditionally where business was conducted, especially where a patron dealt with *clientalia*, his clients or dependants. However, a wealthy noble's *domus* now normally also had extensive *peristyles* (colonnaded courtyards) and proper gardens, that together would have given the space for the social and official activities that even such a modest emperor needed. The best-preserved and halfway comparable villas are at Pompeii and include the House of the Faun or House of the Vettii.

Augustus' *domus* was probably larger than these, with its own libraries. It was right next to the marble temple of Apollo that he had just had built and also near the ancient but carefully preserved hut in which Romulus and Remus had traditionally grown up, so it had a truly imperial location. The so-called House of Livia, which may have belonged to Augustus' wife (who long survived him), was nearby. Later building covered these structures, but they are all visible today.

Tiberius, Augustus' morose successor in AD14, built the Domus Tiberiana before he finally retired to his cliff-top hermitage on Capri in AD27. This was a large rectangular palace 200 by 130yds (180 by 120m) on the north-west side of the Palatine. Built around a vast *peristyle*

court with an oval fishpond, it now lies inaccessible beneath 16th-century gardens. Caligula is thought to have harboured grand designs for extending this palace towards the Forum Romanum but was assassinated before anything was built. His successor Claudius was content to live almost as modestly as Augustus.

NERO'S FIRST PALACE

Almost from the start of his reign in AD 54, Nero, still only 16 years old, wanted to emulate the Hellenistic monarchies' love of culture and regal splendour. As he shed the early inhibitions imbued in him by his tutor, the philosopher-playwright Seneca, he began to build. Nero decided to connect the Domus Tiberiana and other imperial properties on the Palatine and Oppian Hills with a house inherited from his father by a series of linking buildings across the low saddle of land now crowned by the Arch of Titus. This Domus Transitoria (literally Palace of the Passageway) was destroyed in the great fire of AD 64, but some of it has survived to reveal Nero's love of opulent materials, refined if lavish taste and his architects' bold inventiveness.

Traces of his Nymphaeum (Fountain Court) beneath the later Flavian Palace show this was an elongated rectangular building whose open courtyard had ornate shell-shaped fountains along all of one wall. On the other side was a square, raised platform topped by a colonnaded pavilion. Opening off this were suites of rooms – presumably intended for intimate outdoor dinner parties as opposed to the grand public dinners at which emperors often officiated – decorated with marble panellings and vaulted ceilings covered with semi-precious stones, white and gilded stucco and paintings.

Many of the raw materials for this building came from Greece, Asia Minor, Africa and Egypt. Its decorations make very fine examples of what is known (from excavations at Pompeii, buried in AD 79) as the Fourth Style, with a few still in the earlier Third Style.

More remarkable architecturally, and still surviving beneath the platform of Hadrian's later Temple to Venus and Roma, is the domed intersection of two barrel-vaulted corridors, supported on four huge piers and probably lit by an *oculus* (central opening). Such a design anticipates many later buildings, most famously the Pantheon. There were marble pools behind screens of columns in two of the arms and the whole area was opulently decorated, partly in coloured marbles, partly in geometric patterns of semi-transparent glass paste. Nero's extravagance on such wholly personal apartments, as opposed to the public buildings on which Augustus had lavished his wealth, was however only just beginning and prefigured the opulence he would eventually create in his *Domus Aurea* (Golden Palace).

Above: The atrium of the House of Menander at Pompeii. Its murals are very similar to those in the first imperial palaces.

Above: Coin of Nero (ruled AD 54–68), the extravagant yet creative emperor.

NERO'S GOLDEN PALACE

Above: The octagonal dining-room lies in the middle of the markedly symmetrical Esquiline Wing, with other rooms radiating off it. Its domed design was strikingly novel.

Below: A gouache copy of a Domus Aurea wall-painting. The style influenced Renaissance artists such as Raphael and 18th-century architects.

The fire that broke out in the Circus Maximus in June AD64 raged for several days, gutting the Domus Transitoria, Nero's first palace, and three of the city's 14 regions, leaving only four regions untouched. It was one of the greatest of all the recurrent fires in the ancient city's history, but it also provided Nero with an unprecedented opportunity.

While there is no truth in the old stories that he started the fire and then "fiddled while Rome burned" – he was actually at Antium some 30 miles away at the time but hurried back to oversee the fire fighting – Nero could now plan on a scale and with a scope normally reserved for the founders of cities.

Dominating the new Rome was to be Nero's own palace, with immense grounds extending some 300 acres (120ha). He called it the Domus Aurea (Golden Palace). In its design, scale and building techniques, most notably in its use of concrete domes and vaults, it is considered to mark a revolution in Roman architecture.

A BRIEF FLOWERING

Most of the palace had a very brief existence. It was built over or incorporated into later structures such as the Baths of Trajan or the Flavian Amphitheatre by Nero's less extravagant successors. Only some lower rooms survived in the Esquiline wing, which was incorporated into the platform of the Baths of Trajan, to be rediscovered in the Renaissance and influence artists such as Raphael and Giulio Romano, who crawled in to admire and copy them.

These subterranean chambers today appear damp and dark and provide a poor impression of how they must have appeared in their short-lived prime. While the more luxurious types of decoration such as mosaics, marble and stucco veneer have long since vanished, the rooms still have fine wall-paintings with delicate landscapes and architectural motifs. These are mostly executed in the Fourth Style, which is best seen in the well-preserved villas at Pompeii.

The architects of this remarkable complex, which was built in under four years, were Severus and Celer, who had already started, but not completed cutting a canal from Lake Avernus to the Tiber. According to Suetonius, writing about the Domus Aureus early in the 2nd century AD (when it had already mostly vanished), "Its entrance hall was large enough to contain a colossal statue of Nero himself, 120ft high, while its whole area was so great that it had a triple colonnade a mile long. An enormous pool, like the sea, was surrounded by buildings that resembled cities, and by a landscaped park with ploughed fields, vineyards, pastures and woods, where all sorts of domestic and wild animals roamed. Everything in the rest

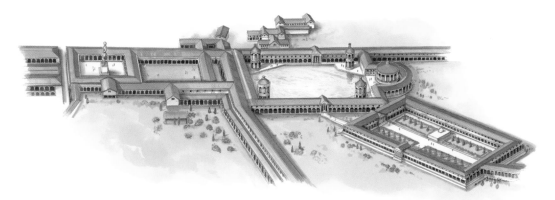

of the palace was inlaid with gold and highlighted with precious stones and mother-of-pearl. The dining-rooms had ceilings with rotating ivory panels which could sprinkle flowers or perfume on guests below. The most remarkable dining-room was circular, its roof rotating day and night like the sky. Sea water or sulphurous water flowed through the baths. When the whole palace had been completed, Nero dedicated it but only remarked, "At last I can begin to live like a human being."

A PALACE IN THE HEART OF A CITY

Nero's walled urban park – about the size of Hyde Park in London, or one third the size of Central Park in New York – was approached from the Forum Romanum along the Via Sacra (Sacred Way), which was straightened and lined with colonnaded porticoes in line with the new regulations for rebuilding all Rome. What angered the Roman people about the new palace was less its ostentatious luxury than the fact that it used so much prime property in the very heart of the city simply for one man's private luxury. A contemporary joke ran, "Rome will become one huge palace, so migrate to Veii [ten miles distant], citizens, until the palace reaches Veii too!" Such open extravagance inside the city contributed to Nero's unpopularity and his downfall within months of the palace's completion in AD68.

Perhaps because the palace was built at breakneck speed – made possible by using brick-faced concrete which was then covered in decorative marble or stucco – the plan of the Domus Aurea is oddly asymmetrical, sometimes even jumbled. The most innovatory of the rooms, which was later incorporated into the platform of the Baths of Trajan, was the octagonal dining-room with rooms radiating off it. The dome had an *oculus* (central opening), while slits let light into the radiating rooms. (This may have been the remarkable dining-room described by Suetonius.) Behind the octagonal room was a jumble of lesser rooms. To the west, at the heart of the palace, was a large pentagonal courtyard which was open to the south and surrounded by a series of major rooms that was flanked by smaller chambers.

As with the rooms opening on to the main courtyard, the architects grouped alternating rectangular rooms, such as the large vaulted dining-room which had screens of columns at both ends, with rooms with apses (semicircular spaces). Of particular note is a barrel-vaulted room off the dining-room, which had a fountain at one end and a mosaic frieze running around the walls made mostly of polychrome glass. The Domus Aurea lived on in public memory as the epitome of extravagant luxury but it also marked a significant development in Roman architecture.

Above: Part of Nero's Domus Aurea, the lavish new palace he built after the Great Fire, with its splendid courts, gardens and colonnades, ate up 300 acres (120ha) of prime urban space in central Rome.

Below: The self-indulgent vanity of this most extravagant of emperors is evident in this bust of Nero.

THE PALATINE: PALACE OF THE EMPERORS

Above: A coloured marble floor from the nymphaeum *of the Domus Transitoria, on the Palatine Hill.*

Below: The courtyard of the nymphaeum *(fountain) in the Domus Flavia, looking towards the basilica from the west side of the main* peristyle.

Vespasian, Nero's successor and founder of the Flavian dynasty, chose the Gardens of Sallust as his house with deliberate modesty; his son Titus (ruled AD79–81) occupied the Domus Tiberiana.

Titus' successor Domitian (ruled AD81–96) was commonly remembered as a tyrant – at least by the Senate and the equestrians, though the army loved him. Undoubtedly, he built grandly in a style befitting the absolute monarchy that the Principate was now becoming.

Domitian's greatest achievement was the palace on the Palatine Hill. This became the emperor's residence for the next three centuries. Praised by the poet Martial for its splendour and size, it was dedicated in AD92. Various repairs were made by several emperors and Septimius Severus added bulky extensions to the eastern and south-western extremities of the palace early in the 3rd century AD. Nonetheless, it remains very much Domitian's monument.

PALACE BUILDINGS

The Domus Aurea had become impractical as an imperial residence for the Flavian dynasty, partly because it was the former palace of the despot Nero and also because, once the Colosseum and Baths of Titus had been built in its park, it was cut off from the main Palatine buildings. Domitian chose Rabirius, a great Roman architect about whose life, typically, nothing is known but who was clearly an inventive genius fond of octagonal and semicircular shapes, to build a completely new palace on the Palatine. The western side of this hill, hallowed by its links with Augustus and Romulus, was already occupied by ancient temples and other venerable buildings, so Rabirius cut a huge terrace in the east ridge which sloped away both south-east and south-west. With the material this produced, he created a flat platform at a higher level to the north.

The palace had two distinct parts: the public audience halls, known as the Domus Flavia, and the private apartments, known as the Domus Augustana. It also had a pleasure garden in the guise of a race track, referred to as a stadium or *hippodromos*, and baths.

There were two main approaches. The official route from the north-east led up the Via Sacra (Sacred Way) and under the arch of Titus into a large paved area, the Area Palatina, which the Domus Flavia overlooked. It was from this approach that the massive bulk of the palace must have looked most imposing. The other route was from the Forum Romanum through a vaulted vestibule. The official wing of the palace, the Domus Flavia, was built on a large platform on

top of the hill with a colonnade round its edge. Behind this colonnade lay three grand state rooms: the Lararium (Chapel to the Lares or household gods); the Aulia Regia (Throne Room) and an apsed basilica.

The Aulia Regia was the largest state room, measuring 98 by 120ft wide (30 by 37m) and very high. Visitors entering by the official, north-east approach would have seen the emperor majestically enthroned beneath a shallow apse at the far end, ready to receive ambassadors and other dignitaries, including Roman senators. This last group regarded being summoned like mere ambassadors as a grievous insult, for they were accustomed to having the emperor come to the Curia (Senate House) to speak to them. Domitian, moreover, insisted on being addressed as *"dominus et deus"* (lord and god), in keeping with his new splendour. This, too, was bitterly resented.

The walls of the throne room were covered with multi-coloured marble while twelve niches held giant statues in black basalt. Free-standing columns of Phrygian marble on tall plinths supported projecting entablatures. The roof, like those elsewhere in the palace, was probably not vaulted but had timber beams. (Whether or not most rooms in the palace had vaulted concrete or straight timber roofs remains a matter of furious debate.) Alongside the throne room there was another grand hall, the basilica, where the emperor heard law cases. It was divided into three by two rows of columns of Numidian yellow marble, which stood forward about 7ft (2m) from the walls, perhaps to allow those waiting to sit on benches. Soon after its construction, the basilica's outer wall began to show signs of subsidence and needed massive buttressing under Hadrian (ruled AD117–38).

THE *TRICLINIUM*

From the throne room visitors passed into the large *peristyle* courtyard. This had a big octagonal pool with a fountain in its centre. Its pink columns of Cappadocian marble, along with its walls of shining white marble were, according to Suetonius, polished like mirrors to let Domitian see any lurking assassins. (The precaution proved useless, for the emperor, who grew increasingly paranoid, was indeed assassinated in the palace.)

A series of semicircular rooms, perhaps official guest bedrooms, lay on the north side of this court, while on the opposite, west side stood the grand *triclinium*, or banqueting hall, called without undue modesty the *Cenatio Iovis* (Jupiter's dining-room). At the far end, a raised apse held the emperor's dining-table, where privileged guests might join him, while spaces for other dining-couches were marked out on the floor. The floor was paved with coloured marble *opus sectile* of purple and green porphyry from Egypt and Greece, *portasanta* from Chios in the Aegean and *giallo antico* from Numidia. The *triclinium* opened on to the courtyard behind a screen of six huge columns of grey Egyptian granite and had five huge windows on each side.

Above: The ruins of the huge columns in the grand triclinium *(dining-room) of the Domus Flavia that Domitian proudly called "Jupiter's dining-room".*

Below: Some of the surviving coloured marble floors of the Domus Flavia, whose lavishness was noted at the time.

Above: Arches from the heavy Severan additions made to the Domus Flavia in the early 3rd century AD.

Below: Although only the brick-faced concrete core of the Domus Flavia has survived, its arches and vaults still rise imposingly on its hill.

THE DOMUS AUGUSTANA

The south-east section of the palace, the domestic wing called the Domus Augustana, was conceived almost as a separate building. Although it covered about twice the area of the Domus Flavia and had three *peristyles* instead of one, for example, it must have seemed less massive from an external viewpoint, except on the side that faced the Circus Maximus. This architectural understatement was perhaps deliberate, for Domitian wanted to advertise public imperial grandeur rather than lavish personal consumption. The Domus Augustana was, in effect, a private villa on a grand scale. In all probability it was very luxurious, but only its lower part has survived to provide clues to its grandeur.

The Domus Augustana was approached from the Area Palatina through a monumental entrance which gave on to a large rectangular *peristyle*, corresponding to that of the Domus Flavia. This led to another *peristyle* with a sunken pool in its centre, whose walls were decorated in Fourth Style paintings. To the south-west lay a maze of small rooms in many different shapes, heights and sizes. Here Rabirius seems to have given his imagination free rein and, far from the public gaze, his imperial patron may have dallied with his harem of concubines, whom he reputedly depilated personally. The puritanism which Domitian tried to enforce in public, most notoriously by reviving the ancient punishment of burial alive for Vestal Virgins who broke their vows of chastity, did not apply inside the palace. Some of these rooms have niches and two are perfect octagons lined with round-headed niches.

A single staircase led from this suite of rooms down to the lower parts of the palace. The staircase was lit by a light-well, at the bottom of which a pool lined with polychrome glass mosaic would have both reflected and coloured the incoming light. Two other light-wells – again over pools whose waters would have reflected and increased the light – lit the surrounding rooms, which included a fine marble-lined *nymphaeum* (fountain room) and another, more intimate *triclinium* (dining-room). Most of these rooms had concrete vaulted ceilings and many were polygonal in shape, reflecting the contemporary prejudice against rectangular shapes. Services such as latrines were hidden discreetly beneath the staircase.

Throughout the Domus Augustana, as in the Domus Flavia, the decorations seem to have been exceptionally rich, with columns, paving and wall veneers of imported, coloured marbles. The few fragments that survive, such as the *opus sectile* floors of the *triclinium*, were made of differently shaped and coloured marbles and formed geometric patterns or pictures. On the walls, mosaics and wall paintings repeated and reinforced the overall impression of sumptuousness. According to Suetonius, however, Domitian was by no means a great gourmet. He normally ate heavily at midday – which was not the usual Roman custom – and contented himself with an apple and a glass of wine in the evening.

OVERLOOKING THE CIRCUS

A passage led from this second *peristyle* into the *hippodromos* or stadium, a sunken garden about 160 by 700ft (50 by 184m) on the palace's south-eastern flank. Lined by a continuous pillared arcade round its two long sides and curved end, it playfully imitated a real circus with mock *carceres* (starting boxes). Trees and pools adorned this most secluded of imperial gardens, with elaborate semicircular fountains at either end.

On the Domus Augustana's south-western façade, overlooking the valley of the Circus Maximus, Rabirius revealed his genius most clearly, for the towering façade curved gently inward with an inter-columnated screen to produce a truly majestic effect, surpassing in external grandeur anything in the Domus Aurea.

If Nero's architects had begun the Roman revolution in architecture by skilfully employing concrete, Rabirius carried it much further. Incorporated in this façade was a *loggia* or imperial box, which the emperor and his entourage could reach directly from the palace. This innovative convenience was subsequently much copied in the later empire.

Above: The ruins of the lower part of the Domus Flavia, with its elaborate, sunken peristyle, courtyard garden. It was built over earlier structures such as Nero's Domus Transitoria, inadvertently preserving them.

Above: A coin of Domitian (ruled AD81–96), the emperor responsible for building most of the palace on the Palatine.

HOUSING FOR RICH AND POOR

As Rome grew richer in the late Republic (from *c.*150BC), the gap between rich and poor was reflected in increasingly divergent standards of housing. Originally most Romans lived in modest *domus* (detached houses). But while the rich inhabited ever more elaborate, spacious *domus*, decorated by artworks and with large gardens adorned with fountains and trees, the not so wealthy increasingly found themselves living, at times precariously, in *insulae*.

Insulae (literally islands) – large, many-storeyed apartment buildings that often took up a whole block – have been called the world's first skyscrapers. A few earlier cities, such as Phoenician Tyre, had had very tall buildings, but *insulae* became the first high buildings to house most of a great city's population and the first to reach (and sometimes breach) height limits of up to 70ft (20m). Initially, these blocks of flats were built very quickly and were in constant danger of fire or collapse. Nero's sensible regulations after the great fire of AD64 helped to improve them, and by AD100 not all *insulae* were slums. Both *domus* and *insulae* were eclipsed by the splendours of the great country villas built by emperors, magnates and other wealthy men across the empire. These have survived better than more modest villas, but are not really typical.

Left: A view of the peristyle *courtyard of the Villa di Poppaea, Oplontis, preserved by Vesuvius in AD79. Its size and splendour are typical of the grander villas of Pompeii.*

THE DOMUS: HOUSES OF THE RICH

Above: The interior of a typical Roman house at Herculaneum, showing how the atrium receives light from above and how the impluvium, *a small reflecting pool, catches the rainwater.*

Below: The peristyle *of the House of the Vettii at Pompeii, the house of a wealthy man, showing its recreated gardens surrounded by typical colonnades.*

The early Roman *domus* (house, from which we derive our word domestic) was a simple, one- or two-storeyed building with rooms set around an *atrium*, a central hall open to the sky. An *impluvium* (pool) in its centre caught rainwater. This type of *domus*, called the Italic house, was derived partly from Etruscan originals. Another larger courtyard, the *peristyle*, was increasingly added to the *domus* in the later Republic. Although both courts grew more grandly colonnaded and decorated, a *domus* typically had mere slits for windows. Often wholly windowless rooms opened off the *atrium* to the outer world, for security rather than privacy.

In Rome, up to the First Punic War (264–241BC), although such houses were the commonest form of dwelling, the *domus* of great patricians were far grander than plebeians' houses. As early as 509BC, the traditional date of the founding of the Republic, there were large houses on the Palatine Hill, with several rooms on more than one floor. Although Roman puritanism, which was strong in the early Republic, long discouraged ostentatious displays of luxury and wealth, houses were nonetheless prized in fashionable areas, preferably close to or in the Forum Romanum, the centre of political life. Bitter rivals among the nobility often had to live side-by-side.

A SOURCE OF DYNASTIC PRIDE

Despite a surprisingly brisk market in Roman property, a *domus* could remain in the same family for generations, sometimes centuries. The patrician Clodius Pulcher, for example, mocked his rival Cicero in 58BC as a *"novus homo"* (literally, new man, one without ancestors in the Senate) for having bought rather than inherited, his house.

When Cicero was temporarily exiled soon after, his house was pulled down to underline his disgrace. By contrast, when the great general Pompey's house passed into Mark Antony's possession after his fall, his trophies were allowed to remain proudly on its walls. The architect Vitruvius, writing *c.* 35BC, observed that, "Distinguished men, required to fulfil their duty by holding public office, must build lofty vestibules in regal style, with spacious atria and peristyles …also libraries and basilicas comparable with magnificent public buildings, because public meetings and private trials take place inside their houses".

Many nobles' houses, with their revered busts of their ancestors, remained intact up to the great fire of AD64 which destroyed much of central Rome. After this, nobles tended to move further from the centre, as life ceased to focus on the Forum Romanum.

The *domus* was therefore never merely a home; it was also a repository of dynastic pride. In addition, its public rooms provided a place for transacting social and

political, rather than commercial, business. Tacitus, writing more than a century after the Republic had ended, still observed that, "The more impressive a man's wealth, house and clothing, the more his name and *clientela* (supporters) become famous". As the nobility's wealth grew, so did the splendours of their *domus*. According to Pliny, the house of Domitius Lepidus, considered the finest in Rome in 78BC, did not even make it into the top 100 only 35 years later.

A visitor to a typical *domus* of the late Republic or early empire would first enter the *atrium*, which was often a room of majestic height. The water in the central *impluvium* helped to diffuse incoming light and to ventilate the surrounding rooms (although it may also have bred malarial mosquitoes). The surrounding rooms were generally simple bedrooms, offices, store-rooms and *alae*, recesses used to store hallowed masks or the busts of family ancestors.

A curtain or wooden screen separated the *atrium* from the *tablinium* (main reception room/office). Beyond lay the *peristyle*, the colonnaded garden around which other rooms were grouped, including open-fronted *exedrae* and often the *triclinium* (dining-room). Only the grander *domus* had proper bathrooms, as many were not connected to mains water and relied instead on rainwater from the *impluvium* or from public fountains. However, the richest displayed their aquatic wealth with elaborate fountains in huge *peristyles*.

The volcanic eruption at Pompeii in AD79 preserved useful physical evidence for all this. However, the *Forma Urbis Romae* (the Severan Marble Map of Rome) also shows a good number of *domus* in the region of the Esquiline and elsewhere.

DECORATIONS

The walls of a *domus* were often brightly painted and the floors covered in mosaics. Thanks to their usually axial layout, which created a vista from the entrance passage through to the *peristyle*, entering visitors would have been dazzled by strong

Mediterranean sunlight alternating with deep shadow. In summer, a *domus* must have been pleasantly cool and airy. In winter, it might have been dark and chilly, with oil lamps shedding feeble light and the only heat provided by smoky braziers. Hypocaust central heating was uncommon except in bathrooms and among the very rich. Glass for windows was also initially uncommon, as it was relatively expensive before the 1st century AD.

The House of the Faun, built *c.* 120BC, in Pompeii is a well-preserved and exceptionally large house of the late Republic. A truly grand *domus*, larger than the contemporary royal palace of Pergamum in Asia Minor, it has a double *atrium* and remarkable mosaics, most famously one showing Alexander the Great's victory at the Issus in 333BC. The subject indicates that Hellenistic influences – which included the *peristyle* itself – had now fused with Italic traditions to create complex, luxurious houses. However, even in Pompeii, which was less heavily populated than Rome, houses were being subdivided by AD79 and the atrium/peristyle house was becoming confined to the very rich.

Above: The atrium in the House of the Mosaic Atrium at Herculaneum shows both the typically fine black-and-white mosaic floor that gave the house its name and the alternation of light and shade through the axis of the house.

Above: Detail of mosaic of Alexander the Great, from the House of the Faun, Pompeii.

Above: Brick-faced concrete was the normal building material used in Rome and, as here, in Ostia for both insulae, *the apartment blocks, and shopping markets.*

Below: While many earlier insulae *were jerry-built, by the 2nd century AD solidly constructed apartment blocks with internal courtyards or gardens were becoming common in Ostia, Rome and other cities. They have lasted impressively well.*

INSULAE: THE FIRST APARTMENT BLOCKS

By *c.* AD150, as Rome's population peaked at probably more than one million, many of its inhabitants were living in *insulae.* This translates literally as islands, although not all actually occupied a whole block of their own. According to the mid-4th century catalogue, there were 46,600 *insulae* in Rome and only 1,790 *domus.* These blocks of flats rose to five, six, even at times seven storeys. Augustus and later Trajan tried to limit their height to 60 and then to 70 ft, but the reiteration of such regulations suggests that such laws had only a limited effect.

LIFE IN AN *INSULA*
Juvenal, the satirical poet, provides a vivid, unflattering but not impartial portrayal of life in an *insula.* "We live in a city supported mostly by slender props, which is how the bailiff patches cracks in old walls, telling the residents to sleep peacefully under roofs ready to fall down around them. No, no I have to live somewhere where there are no fires or alarms every night ... if the alarm is sounded on the ground floor the last man to be burnt alive will be the one with nothing to shelter him from the rain but the roof tiles."

Some *insula* blocks survive in Rome, but most evidence comes from Ostia, whose remains show that in fact, many apartments on lower floors were very habitable, even comfortable. Some first-floor apartments had running water and large, possibly glazed windows.

Spacious apartments, with separate rooms for dining and sleeping, were inhabited by wealthy citizens, including some equestrians (knights) and even senators, perhaps as friends of the usually aristocratic owner. Often such wealthier tenants paid rent annually and had some security of tenure. In contrast, garrets under the tiles up many flights of stairs must have been cramped, hot in summer, cold in winter, insalubrious without toilets or water and dangerous because of the fires that repeatedly ravaged Rome. Here tenants paid by the week or even day and faced the constant threat of eviction. However, all lived in the same building, the rich beneath the poor, in a pattern repeated in many great cities before the advent of lifts.

Insulae are first recorded surprisingly early – in 218BC an ox climbed two floors up one before falling, according to Livy – but they really developed in the last century of the Republic (from 133BC) as the city's population exploded. At first they were mainly jerry-built, with thin walls of mud-brick and upper floors made mostly of wood. Crassus, notoriously the richest man in mid-1st century BC Rome, made his fortune in property speculation. He would turn up with his gang of fire-fighting slaves when an *insula* caught

fire, commiserate with the bereft owner and buy up the smouldering site cheap for redevelopment at greater density. However, even the high-minded Cicero owned *insulae* which he admitted were unsafe but which brought him the sizeable income of 80,000 sesterces. Rome was less a city of owner-occupiers than one of a few great landlords, with their dependants and friends, and of many harassed, poorer tenants. This hierarchy was typical of Roman society.

TYPICAL *INSULAE*

After the great fire of AD64, new building regulations – which were not universally enforced but which still provide a useful guide – stipulated that *insulae* be built of brick-faced concrete, with balconies or arcades for fire-fighters.

One of the few substantially surviving *insulae* in Rome is on the Via Giulio Romano (named after the Renaissance painter) at the foot of the Capitoline Hill. It is a typical *insula* with shops on the ground floor and residential mezzanines (half floors) above. The first floor proper was occupied by two decent-sized apartments, and its second and third floors by flats with smaller rooms, most with concrete vaults. There are traces of at least two more floors above (the Capitoline Museum now above it precludes further

archaeological investigation), which probably became progressively more cramped. Another *insula* built under Hadrian (ruled AD117–38) has been discovered beneath the Galleria Colonna with shops, some with back rooms, on all four sides on the ground floor. On the west side, facing the ancient Via Lata, was an arcade which reached to the adjoining buildings, obeying Nero's fire regulations. Separate flats occupied its upper floors and were reached by their own staircases. One *insula*, the Felicula built in the 2nd century AD, was so imposing that it became one of the famous sights of Rome, alongside the Colosseum and Trajan's Forum.

However, the best-preserved *insulae* are in Ostia. This city grew into a boom-town after Trajan constructed a new harbour at nearby Portus but was later completely abandoned to the river silt. Here, solid buildings of brick-faced concrete with fine depressed brick arches often faced on to courtyards or communal gardens, with shops on the street side and light-wells on the other. Staircases rose up to apartments above, some of which had balconies and fine wall paintings, as in the House of Diana. This complex of shops and living areas was at least three storeys high, with a communal toilet for nine or ten people. The overall effect is surprisingly modern.

Above: A reconstruction of a typical block of flats in Ostia, probably built soon after AD100. The ground floor would have contained shops with mezzanines above, and the first floor above that could have held spacious, even comfortable apartments.

Below: Ostia boomed after Trajan built a new harbour at Portus, but the Romans always built to last, as the state today of these massive brick-faced piers attests.

TIBERIUS' VILLA AT CAPRI

Outside the city of Rome, emperors could build more grandly and freely. Augustus acquired the small island of Capri, which retained some of its original Greek-speaking inhabitants, and built a relatively modest seaside villa there, the Palazzo a Mare. Tiberius (ruled AD14–37) was Augustus' uncontested successor, but his was a hard act to follow.

Above: Tiberius, Augustus' charmless successor, inherited his power but not his tact, and finally withdrew to Capri.

Below: Tiberius chose a markedly inaccessible site 1,000ft (300m) above the sea for his main villa on Capri.

RETREAT FROM ROME
While Augustus had mellowed into a tactful, deeply revered *pater patriae* (father of his country), Tiberius became embittered by the perceived repeated snub of being passed over in the succession in favour first of Augustus' son-in-law and then of his grandsons. By the time Tiberius assumed power, he was in his fifties. He

had a fine military record, great dynastic pride – his family, the Claudii, were grander than the Julii – but also a morose, cynical temperament that gradually emerged from beneath a hypocritical veneer of Republican virtue (or so wrote Tacitus a century later).

Tiberius came to hate living in Rome where his position was awkwardly anomalous: in theory he was *primus inter pares* (first among equals) in a Republic, in practice he was absolute monarch. In AD22, after the death of his only son Drusus, he moved to a villa on the Campanian coast, and in AD27 finally withdrew to Capri. Roman officials now had to go to this relatively inaccessible if beautiful island in the Bay of Naples to consult their emperor. Their journey was made worse by the security precautions that Sejanus, Tiberius' Praetorian Prefect, erected around his master. (Sejanus' own imperial ambitions – he wanted to marry into the imperial family and create his own dynasty – led to his downfall in AD31.)

Tiberius owned 12 properties on Capri, of which by far the most important was the Villa Jovis (Villa of Jupiter), vertiginously sited on the island's eastern promontory 1,000ft (300m) above the Tyrrhenian Sea. It was not a spacious site and, being so high, the water supply was a major problem, but it satisfied the ageing emperor's two main desires for security and privacy. Capri was noted for having few beaches suitable for landing and very high cliffs.

At the heart of the villa was a rectangular courtyard around 100ft (30m) square, probably covered with mosaics and surrounded by colonnades. Beneath it was a network of massive vaulted cisterns that collected every drop of water from Capri's infrequent but heavy rainfall. Built around this were four separate wings at different levels. These were

linked by staircases and ramps. At the south-west corner lay the entrance vestibule with the guard house; along the south side was a suite of baths; along the west side, built up against the sheer outer face of the cistern block, were rooms for the courtiers and officials on three floors. On the east was a large semi-circular state hall flanked by similar reception rooms and on the north flank, accessible only by a single, well-guarded corridor and almost separate from the rest of the palace, lay the relatively modest quarters of the emperor himself.

Richly decorated, the emperor's quarters opened on to a sheltered loggia below, with steps leading up to a belvedere with stunning views over the Bay of Naples. Here the emperor would walk after his evening meals in the *triclinium* (dining-room), which had coloured marble floors. The unknown architect exploited the site to magnificent effect, allowing the emperor to withdraw from the world to a waterless cliff-top and yet still enjoy his luxurious Roman baths.

UNQUIET SECLUSION

Approaching not on the meandering, tree-lined track that the modern tourist takes, but by a herring-bone brick paved road ascending abruptly from the west, a Roman visitor would have seen the palace rising an impressive 60ft (18m) above the hilly ground. Tiberius seldom welcomed visitors, however, and grew increasingly paranoid in his later years.

Such seclusion fuelled ugly rumours that Suetonius later happily collated and reported as historical facts. Among these was the story of the fisherman who climbed up the cliffs to present the emperor with an exceptional mullet he had caught. This so alarmed the security-mad Tiberius that he ordered his guards to rub the scaly fish in the man's face until he bled. Tiberius also delighted in having victims thrown off the cliffs from his palace, while sailors waited at the bottom with boat hooks to finish off survivors. Although in his seventies, Tiberius, wrote

Suetonius, became sexually depraved in his old age: "Collecting bevies of boys and girls from all over the empire, adepts in unnatural practices, to copulate in front of him in threesomes to stimulate his jaded appetites. Many rooms were filled with obscene pictures … he further had boys and girls dress up as Pan and nymphs to prostitute themselves in front of caves or grottoes".

One man whom Tiberius continued to trust was Thrasyllus, his chief astrologer, for astrology, along with Greek literature and mythology, was one of Tiberius' life-long interests. Symbolically, a light house on Capri that Tiberius used to signal to the mainland was struck by lightning and destroyed shortly before the emperor's death (probably from natural causes) in AD37. News of the reclusive ruler's demise was rapturously received in Rome and his villa at Capri was soon abandoned.

Above: The walkway from the Great Hall in the Villa Jovis, showing construction in concrete with opus incertum facing and brick course.

Below: Part of the massive wall of the substructure of Tiberius' villa, made of reticulate facing with fired brick bands.

HADRIAN'S VILLA AT TIVOLI

Above: Portrait bust of the emperor Hadrian. The most peripatetic, cultured and cosmopolitan of emperors, Hadrian created at Tivoli a villa of unparalleled size and luxury where he could both recall his travels and summon the empire's ruling classes.

Below: Model of the villa-complex at Tivoli, showing the Piazza d'Oro at its centre. The grandest of imperial residences, the villa in many ways witnessed the climax of Roman architecture with its boldly, even astonishingly innovatory, curved shapes.

Hadrian followed Nero in being a great builder and a passionate philhellene (admirer of Greek culture), but similarities end there. While Nero was an increasingly debauched playboy and would-be artist who neglected affairs of state, Hadrian was an excellent soldier and tireless administrator, traversing the empire and founding cities or fortifications from Egypt to Britain, where he built his renowned Wall.

A MUCH FAVOURED SPOT

Although Hadrian was among the finest emperors Rome ever had, paradoxically, he did not much like the city of Rome itself. He got on badly with the Senate, four of whose most senior members were summarily executed at the start of Hadrian's reign on dubious charges of treachery, possibly on his orders. Nor was he popular with the Roman people, who preferred their emperors less openly cultured. (He was contemptuously nick-named *Graeculus*, "Little Greek", by the upper classes.) However, his reputation with the army, administration (including

the equestrian order) and the provinces – with troubled Palestine perhaps the one exception – remained unshakeable.

The huge villa-palace Hadrian built at Tivoli (Tibur) some 20 miles (32km) east of Rome, where he spent most of his last years, did not rouse the same disapproval as Nero's Golden Palace precisely because it was *outside* the city. The area had long been a favourite beauty spot and the poets Catullus and Horace and the emperor Trajan had owned villas there, but for Hadrian it marked no hermit-like retreat from public life to the *campagna* (countryside). Instead, the highest members of Rome's increasingly cosmopolitan governing class came to his villa-palace both to discuss affairs of state and to be imperially entertained. Tivoli remains the most radical, intriguing and grandiose of Roman villas. Its buildings cover an area of around 300 acres (120ha) and stretch nearly half a mile (800m) along a plateau.

AN ARCHITECTURAL CLIMAX

The period of the villa's probably inter-mittent construction (c. AD118–33) is sometimes considered to mark the climax of the Roman revolution in architecture, when the design of a building's interior came to dictate its overall shape. It certainly shows the keen interest of Roman architects at the time in curvilinear forms, which produced some of the most remarkable of all Roman buildings.

The villa, which was some distance from Rome, had to be big enough to accommodate the emperor's entourage – soldiers, servants, bureaucrats and courtiers – but it also provided Hadrian with the opportunity to recreate, imaginatively rather than exactly, some parts of the empire that had appealed to him. In this he was following Roman precedents but on a much grander scale. The layout, which deliberately juxtaposed conflicting

axes to follow the lie of the ground, was influenced by earlier villas' landscaped gardens. This produced what initially seems a haphazard appearance but one that worked well with, rather than against, the contours of the land. The palace and its gardens were unwalled although guarded, for Hadrian was no recluse.

Construction of the complex probably began around the Republican-era villa owned by the Empress Sabina, Hadrian's unloved wife. A pre-existing grotto with fountain and *cryptoporticus* (basement or subterranean vaulted corridor) was incorporated into the new villa around what became the library court and Hadrian's private suite.

Among the main structures was the *poikile*, a huge *peristyle* courtyard measuring about 250 by 110yds (230 by 100m) with a large pool in its centre. Substantial buttressing with rows of concrete barrel vaults was needed at its west end to produce the required flat area. These vaults then provided rooms for guards or servants. All four sides are lined with colonnades and the two shorter ends are curved like Trajan's Forum, which had been built only a few years before.

It was once thought that the *poikile* was a careful reproduction of the *stoa poikile*, (painted colonnade) in Athens, which gave its name to the Stoic school of philosophers who met there. However, the recently excavated Athenian Stoa does not really resemble it and the complex was more probably an imitation of either Aristotle's Lyceum or Plato's Academy.

The central part of the *poikile* was arranged as a *dromos* (race-track). From the east of this *dromos*, visitors could pass through an apsed library into the Island Villa, the so-called Teatro Marittimo (Maritime theatre) set within a circular moat, crossed by bridges, around which ran a barrel-vaulted passage supported by white Ionic columns. This is perhaps the most original building in the whole highly original palace, without a single straight line in it. Instead, an amazing mixture of convex and concave chambers face on to a

miniature courtyard with a small fountain, whose conch-shaped plan echoes that of the surrounding rooms, which are themselves arranged in four curved groups. Here the emperor could retreat from the state business of the rest of his palace and devote himself to literature (he was a poet) or to other relaxations, soothed by the sound of running waters and by their sparkling in the sunlight which they reflected into the shaded rooms around. A small bath house and latrines were secreted within the building, along with a suite of bedrooms.

PUMPKIN VAULTS

The motif of curve and counter-curve is repeated in the Piazza d'Oro (Golden Square), as the richly decorated *peristyle* court is now known because of the surviving gold-yellow mosaics on the floor of its colonnades. It was entered from the north through an octagonal vestibule with niches on seven of its sides. The whole room was covered by an eight-sided umbrella vault, the famous "pumpkin vaults" supposedly criticized by Trajan's great architect Apollodorus. Opposite, on the south-east side, stands a larger pavilion or *nymphaeum*, that was octagonal with alternately concave and convex sides.

Above: The Maritime Theatre, or Island Villa, offered the busy emperor a retreat from affairs of state.

Below: Floor mosaics retain some of the gold that explains the name Piazza d'Oro.

Above: Caryatids, modelled on Greek originals, line the Canopus, a waterway recalling the canal near Alexandria in Egypt. They are a typical example of Hadrian's highly original, even capricious, eclecticism.

(Second-century AD Roman architecture has sometimes been called baroque because of such complex and dynamic shapes.) The Corinthian columns of this building and courtyard were of white marble and some have been re-erected. In the centre of the *peristyle* was another long pool.

THE IMPERIAL APARTMENTS

The largest group of buildings at Tivoli lay south-west of the Piazza d'Oro. This included the *triclinium* (state dining-room), stadium (or hippodrome) and what were probably the main imperial apartments, which were approached by a single staircase. These combined to form a single, imposing block.

The rooms west of the secluded court have the villa's best views – St Peter's in Rome is now visible from them – and the only hypocaust heating of the villa, suggesting they were inhabited by the emperor himself.

The *triclinium* on the far side of the stadium is half open with three *exedrae*, each with a semicircular garden, while the fourth side has a large ornate fountain whose roar must have soothed diners. Domitian's palace in Rome was the obvious inspiration for this. The *triclinium*'s walls were covered in white Proconnesian marble with remarkably elaborate columns. Beyond were two sets of baths: the Small Baths were probably for the emperor's personal use and their design was again curvilinear to suit the site. The Large Baths are more conventional but have an impressive vaulted *frigidarium* (cold bath) with Ionic columns. To their west is a circular room, the *heliocaminus* or sun room, whose tall windows faced south-west to capture the sun's heat.

MEMENTOES OF TRAVELS

The Canopus/Serapeum complex directly north of the baths most obviously recalls Hadrian's travels in Egypt. The lake, 130yds (119m) long, resembles in miniature the canal from Canopus to Alexandria and is lined with copies of Greek and Egyptian statues, while the

The four convex sides gave on to four remarkably shaped rooms, each of which ended in a semicircular *exedra*. Two of the concave sides open on to small summer rooms with fountains in their centres, while one formed the entrance. On the opposite side, the other wall led into a large semi-circular *nymphaeum* whose dramatically curving back wall was lined with alternately round and square fountain niches. The whole pavilion must have been filled with the sound of jetting waters and lit up by the sunlight reflected off them.

Above: A figure of a river or sea god reclining near the Canopus. One of the numerous Greek statues copied at Tivoli.

semicircular half-domed *nymphaeum* at its end recreates, again in miniature, the Serapeum, the temple to Serapis in Alexandria. A special aqueduct supplied the whole villa. Beyond the Serapeum lay the Academy, a mainly open-air, octagonally shaped building. An exact copy of the Temple of Venus on the Greek island of Cnidos is among the other buildings which adorn the grounds.

STATUES AND PAINTINGS

If the villa Hadrian built at Tivoli was architecturally radical, the sculptures and paintings he chose to decorate it were artistically conservative or nostalgic. The caryatids lining the Canopus look back –

beyond Augustus' own neoclassical use of them for his Forum over a century before – to the 5th century BC originals of the Erechtheum on the Athenian Acropolis. Other statues at Hadrian's villa are also copies of famous Greek originals and some of the mosaics are copies of famous classical Greek artworks. For example, the *Centauromachia* (Battle of the Centaurs) imitates a painting by Zeuxis of almost 500 years earlier.

Such emulation, common among Romans of many classes, was especially marked in Hadrian's reign, which witnessed the movement called the Second Sophistic. This, one of many neoclassical revivals in Rome's history, was a deliberate attempt to recreate the styles, manners and even debates of classical Greece in its 5th-century BC heyday.

The villa at Tivoli shows the resources of the whole empire devoted to realizing the grand vision of a man of exceptional talent and originality – this was probably the emperor himself, who is thought to have quarrelled with and exiled Apollodorus – using the latest techniques of Roman concrete and vaulting. Plundered repeatedly after the collapse of the empire, its marble stolen or burnt to make lime for cement, the Villa has been partially restored in recent decades to recall a few of its former wonders.

Above: The Baths of the Heliocaminus, a circular sun room whose tall south-west-facing windows would have caught the afternoon sun and so helped to heat the chamber.

Below: Intersecting vaulted corridors with skylights. These ran beneath the villa complex and gave access to the rooms built into the substructure where the emperor's many guards and other attendants were quartered.

VILLAS OF THE RICH IN ITALY

Above: Typical of the many opulent villas built on the shores of the Bay of Naples in the 1st centuries BC and AD is the Villa di Poppaea at Oplontis, near Herculaneum. It was preserved for posterity by the eruption of Vesuvius.

Below: This landscape fresco imaginatively but not perhaps unrealistically depicts villas with fine colonnades, porticoes and gardens looking out over the Bay of Naples.

If no other villa approached Hadrian's in lavish inventiveness or size, many wealthy nobles built themselves remarkably fine villas across the empire, most especially in Italy. A villa in the Republic meant a country house, increasingly comfortable perhaps, but still the centre of a working agricultural estate with farm buildings often attached, as they were with Palladio's Renaissance "villas" in the Veneto much later. They were not mere pleasure pavilions, as the writings of Cato and Varro attest. By the 1st century AD, however, elaborate villas were being built solely for the relaxation of wealthy Romans. Seaside villas – for wealthy but not necessarily noble owners – were common around the Bay of Naples, the Roman "Riviera". Such villas often had slender, elongated pillars, broken pediments and elaborate sun terraces and colonnades looking out to sea. These were depicted in the murals in the House of Lucretius

Fronto of the mid-1st century AD. These murals are now thought to depict actual houses, if perhaps imaginatively. This Roman love of the seaside was not to recur before 18th-century England invented seabathing and it testifies to the peacefulness of the Mediterranean, the empire's inland sea. The greatest Roman villas in Italy were mostly built further north. These very large, luxurious structures are the exception rather than the rule. Many villas in Italy were much smaller and far less luxurious, but still relatively opulent and well-appointed.

THE VILLA OF PLINY THE YOUNGER

Few villas had such an interesting owner as Pliny the Younger (c. AD61–112), the genial man of letters, senator, consul and friend of the emperor Trajan, who ended his career as proconsul (governor) of Bithynia in Asia Minor.

Pliny had two villas which he used as retreats from urban business, one near Rome at Laurentum, the other, larger one in Tuscany at Tifernum. As he confessed in one letter, beautiful surroundings were the first thing Pliny looked for in a villa, although he was also a conscientious landowner, overseeing his mostly tenanted farms. (They brought him in a huge 400,000 sesterces a year.)

Pliny's writings about his villa, with its large glazed windows, heated bath houses, formal gardens filled with statues and topiary, *triclinia* (dining-rooms), libraries and picturesque site, later influenced houses from the Renaissance on, especially in Georgian England. In it, Pliny could enjoy *otium cum dignitate*, the cultured, dignified leisure that was the Roman ideal. His villa was conservative in style, however, for it retained, on an expanded scale, the *atrium/peristyle* plan *"ex more veterum"* (in the old manner) as he expressed it.

More radical architecturally was the so-called Grotte di Catulle (Grottoes of Catullus), although the great poet had nothing to do with the building erected long after his death except for the fact that he, too, had once owned a villa on Lake Garda. The huge villa, built for an unknown but wealthy Roman on the northern tip of the peninsula of Sirmione, which juts into the lake, probably dates from the early 2nd century AD. It exploits concrete in a way which suggests that the architect was aware of recent developments in Rome, which included Domitian's Domus Flavia.

A huge platform was built over massive concrete vaults at the villa's northern end, offering superb views of the lake and mountains. Its plan was severely rectilinear, consisting of a great central block 590ft long and 345ft wide (180 by 105m). Roughly symmetrical, it had rectangular, almost block-like *exedrae* at each end. The rooms were grouped around the vast *peristyle* court, although the *tricilinia* probably looked out over the lake to allow diners to enjoy the views. Roman appreciation of such dramatic natural beauty anticipates that of the Romantics by almost 17 centuries.

A LUXURY SURBURBAN VILLA

Many Roman nobles preferred to build their luxurious villas closer to Rome. Typical of these is the Villa of Sette Bassi, only 6 miles (10km) south of Rome on the Via Latina and therefore almost suburban in location.

The villa seems to be the result of three separate phases of construction, carried out with typically Roman speed between AD140 and 160. In the first phase its plan was conventional enough, with a modest residential section ranged along the south side of a large *peristyle*. This first villa was mostly single-storeyed, with a simple exterior. Not long after its completion, a second wing was added on the west of the entrance *peristyle*. This required the construction of terraces on concrete substructures, a rather more adventurous

project, if on a smaller scale. On the southern side of the new west façade projected a semicircular veranda with a fountain in the centre of a colonnade courtyard. The surface of the supporting terrace was topped by shallow segmental arches on brackets of travertine stone similar to contemporary *maeniana* (balconies) in Trajan's Market in Rome.

In the third and most complex phase of building, a wing was built across the north end of the area west of the older buildings and a huge *cryptoporticus* (underground vaulted corridor) about 1,000ft (300m) long enclosed the whole complex as a formal terraced garden. A massive new north wing, built on terraced vaults, rose at least three storeys, with two immense, tall reception halls with triple windows and gabled roofs. These halls were lit from above in a way developed by later Roman architects.

Buildings of such scale must have been hugely expensive, affordable only to the wealthiest of aristocrats. It is possible that the villa was built by a senator who wanted to keep a safe distance from the imperial court, but this was exactly the sort of lavish suburban villa the debauched emperor Commodus (AD180–92) later expropriated for orgies.

Above: The Grotte di Catulle is a splendid villa of c. AD120 at Sirmione, but it is not connected with Catullus.

Below: The House of Marcus Loreius Tiburtinus at Pompeii. Some of the fine and elaborate decorations that once covered the building still survive.

VILLAS OF THE EMPIRE: PIAZZA ARMERINA

Above: One of the villa's fanciful and colourful mosaics shows a putto or cupid in the god Neptune's entourage riding a sea monster.

Below: A huge peristyle, with a fountain, gardens and paths decorated with mosaics, lay at the heart of the villa.

In the centre of Sicily, once one of the empire's most fertile provinces, lie the ruins of one of the grandest Roman villas. Now listed as a UNESCO World Heritage Site, the villa dates from the early 4th century AD, a period when the empire had partly recovered from the turmoil of the 3rd century under the iron leadership of Diocletian (ruled AD284–305).

Luxurious and complex, the villa boasts such remarkably fine and extensive mosaics – they cover nearly 400,000sq ft (35,000sq m) – that it was long thought to have belonged to Maximian, Diocletian's co-emperor, who retired to Sicily. It was called the Villa Imperiale.

Today, the imperial connection is doubted and the owner is thought to have been a very wealthy member of the Roman aristocracy. It is thought possible that he had estates in North Africa – the greatest Roman families had estates in many parts of the empire – for the villa's plan suggests African influences. Whoever the owner was, he clearly enjoyed a life

unclouded by threats from barbarians, for the villa is rambling and unwalled, unlike Diocletian's compact fortress-palace at Split of slightly earlier origin. It seems that the owner was also unconcerned by the rise of Christianity, for the scenes in the mosaics are sensually and exuberantly pagan, revelling in hunting, mythological and bathing scenes.

LOOKING INWARD

The villa is made up of four connected groups of buildings, probably constructed between AD310 and 330 on the site of a modest 2nd-century AD villa. The overall irregularity of its plan in some ways recalls the planned informality of Hadrian's Tivoli villa, but at Piazza Armerina there is no attempt to relate the buildings to the landscape. This suggests that its owner preferred to look in on his own elaborate decorations rather than out at the natural world beyond.

Piazza Armerina is typical of late Roman buildings in the way that the design of the interiors dominates that of the exteriors. The suite of bath houses, for example, was planned as a series of inter-connected interiors and creates a jumbled effect from outside. However, the overall plan reveals a unity of design which suggests that a single mind may have been behind the entire project.

The villa may have been inhabited as late as AD900 – Sicily was reconquered by the Byzantines in AD535 and remained in their hands for more than 400 years. In the 12th century the whole area was covered by an immense mudslide. This destroyed most of its walls but preserved the mosaics both from the elements and from vandalism. Excavations only began in 1881 and are still continuing. Some of the pillars have been restored and, in a few areas, walls rise high enough to reveal the layout very clearly.

Left: Part of the Great Hunt Mosaic in the ambulatory or hall of the villa. These mosaics, which are very well preserved, are Piazza Armerina's crowning glory and rejoice in exuberant scenes of life and death. Here, a lion kills a deer.

Approaching through a monumental triple arch into a horseshoe-shaped entrance courtyard to the west, Roman visitors would have turned right into the main part of the villa. This consisted of an enfilade of rooms: a vestibule gave on to a massive *peristyle* with living quarters around it. Beyond this, approached by a small staircase, lay a transverse corridor about 200ft (63m) long, now known as the Ambulatory of the Great Hunt Scene.

Beyond the walkway was a large hall with an apse at its far end. At the south end lay the private wing with a tiny semicircular *sigma* (courtyard). This had two bedroom suites and a small *triclinium* (dining-room). South of this was another ceremonial wing with a large trilobed *triclinium*. The substantial baths complex projected obliquely to the north-west of the *peristyle*. The nearby latrine was typically elegant, with a brick drain, marble wash basin and lavish mosaics.

GLOWING WITH COLOUR

The greatest glory of the Piazza Armerina lies underfoot in its superb mosaics, which still glow with colour after their centuries under 30ft (9m) of preserving mud.

Probably the work of craftsmen from Africa, they give an extraordinarily vivid picture of life in the later empire, at least as enjoyed by the very rich. The transverse corridor is also more poetically called the Ambulatory of the Great Hunt Scene because it has the finest mosaics. These show figures in imperial-looking capes watching a remarkable scene in which all sorts of animals – leopards, tigers, elephants, ostriches, antelopes and a rhino – are being caught and loaded on to a ship, presumably for transport to Rome to be slaughtered in the games.

West of the main *peristyle* in the *palaestra* (gymnasium), mosaics show detailed and informative scenes of games in the Circus Maximus in Rome. The owner probably sponsored these games in a typical form of aristocratic patronage. A smaller room to the *peristyle*'s south is the aptly named Room of the Ten Girls. Here, colourful mosaics depict girls wearing what may be the world's first bikinis. The mosaics in total are a splendid manifestation of the still vibrant and sensual pagan world, although their rather flattened style points to the emergence of a new, late Roman-early Byzantine art.

Below: The world's first bikinis? These mosaics, in the well-named Room of the Ten Girls, show girls wearing jewellery but not much else, dancing, exercising and swimming in bathing costumes that look surprisingly modern.

DIOCLETIAN'S PALACE AT SPLIT

Above: The steely resolution of Diocletian, who established the tetrarchy and, uniquely among Roman emperors, retired peacefully.

Below: The Golden Gate, the main entrance to Diocletian's fortress-palace, was ornamental and functional. Its statues in niches hint at Syrian influences.

Diocletian (ruled AD284–305) was unique among Roman emperors in retiring peacefully – traditionally to grow cabbages in his garden – before dying in bed six years later. Equally unusual was his retirement home. Far from being a luxurious villa in Italy, it was a massive fort enclosing a palace on the Adriatic coast at Split (Spalato), now in Croatia. Its military plan testifies not just to Diocletian's life in the army – in fact, he was more an administrative reformer than a brilliant soldier – but to the general insecurity of the age.

While Split was far enough from any frontier, barbarians had, within living memory, penetrated even into central Italy, the heart of the empire. Diocletian may not have completely trusted his successors in the tetrarchy, his carefully designed system of four emperors, either.

As it was, his retirement was disturbed only by calls for him to mediate between his quarrelling heirs, which he did only once, in AD308, without success. It is possible the huge walls he constructed helped to deter would-be aggressors. They later sheltered the whole of the small town's population for many centuries and still stand substantially intact today.

DOMESTIC MEETS MILITARY STYLE
Built AD300–6, the palace is halfway between a self-contained, fortified country residence of a type becoming common across the increasingly troubled empire, and a small town. Its overall plan, however, recalls a typical Roman army camp. It is rectangular – 590 by 710ft (180 by 216m) – with square towers in each corner, six further square towers along the walls and

octagonal towers flanking the three land entrances. Two intersecting colonnaded streets divide the palace into four sections. On the seaward side, the wall was surmounted by a gallery of arches flanked by columns, the whole facade unbroken apart from one small postern gate giving access to the quays. That part of the Dalmatian coast is relatively inaccessible by land, and Diocletian must have relied on ships to supply him with the news and other necessaries that were required for his imperial retirement.

The palace's northern parts formed barracks for the imperial guard that Diocletian retained, while the southern two sections, built out on terraces over lower ground, formed the palace's residential and state apartments. These have not yet been fully excavated. The southern end of the street forms the so-called *Peristyle* and is flanked by still impressive arched colonnades with a huge broken-pedimented end wall. To the west of this street lay a small temple and to the east an octagonal mausoleum, that was circular inside. The *Peristyle* led to a circular vestibule, beyond which was a large rectangular hall, presumably a state reception room. This gave on to the corridor flanked by the line of arches overlooking the sea, and was itself flanked by two further state rooms.

Although in retirement, Diocletian maintained much of the almost hieratic splendour with which he had surrounded the throne. The western hall had an apse at one end and was probably a throne room; the eastern hall was probably the *triclinium* (dining-room). Beyond these halls on each side lay domestic suites with bedrooms and bath houses.

THE PALACE'S PRECEDENTS
It has been suggested that the palace's layout derives partly from Diocletian's palace at Antioch – which he had built on the other side of the River Orontes on a site first occupied by the emperor Valerian in AD259 – and partly from the city-palace of Philippopolis in southern

Syria, the birthplace of the emperor Philip the Arab (ruled AD244–9). Diocletian, although born in the Balkans, had spent most of his reign governing the East and would have had the opportunity to see and even to occupy both. The extreme regularity of the plan more obviously recalls the roughly contemporary Baths of Diocletian in Rome.

Architects and craftsmen from Syria and other Eastern provinces were probably employed in building Split. Typical of this Syrian influence are the arcuated lintel – an arched entablature over the centre of a classical façade – and the arcaded columns of the *Peristyle*. The main entrance, the Porta Aurea (Golden Gate), also reveals Eastern influences. Its open arch with horizontal lintel and its decorative front with statues in niches were probably inspired by the Temple of Bacchus at Baalbek, built 150 years before. However, more recent, Western influences are apparent too, such as the circular vestibule and the framing of the seafront gallery's arches between decorative half-columns, a device also employed in the Mausoleum of Maxentius outside Rome and the grand Porta Nigra at Trier.

The palace's thick walls enclose courtyard gardens where the elderly emperor could have strolled and done some gardening. But the monumental architecture, while undoubtedly palatially opulent, is distinctly heavy. The final effect is both impressive and oppressive, rather like Diocletian's imperial regime itself.

Above: An imaginative reconstruction of how the palace looked in its prime, c. AD306. It was mainly supplied by sea.

Below: Diocletian built an elaborate mausoleum for himself that was later turned into a cathedral, while his palace became a town.

VILLAS OF THE EMPIRE: BRITISH VILLAS

Above: The larger and more luxurious Roman villas made great use of hypocausts (underfloor) and intramural hot-air heating, as in this villa at Chedworth. This was the first and almost the last form of central heating in Britain until the 20th century.

Below: Cupid rides a dolphin in a fine mid-2nd-century AD floor mosaic from Fishbourne Palace. Built c. AD75, the Sussex villa was palatial in size and luxury if not in name.

Britain, part of the Roman empire for nearly four centuries, soon became far more than a mere frontier province, and today is recognized as having been wealthier and more Romanized than was once thought. Unlike villas nearer the Mediterranean, British villas were not usually built around a *peristyle* but tended to be "winged corridor" types, with wings of rooms added incrementally, almost accidentally and sometimes forming courts. If most Roman villas in Britain (as elsewhere) remained modestly rustic, a few developed into grand houses of a scale and complexity not seen again in Britain until at least the 16th century.

THE PALACE AT FISHBOURNE
The first great villa – in every way atypically grandiose because of its royal and imperial links – is the palace at Fishbourne on the Sussex coast. It may have belonged to the client king Cogidubnus, king of the Regnenses. Alternatively, it could have been the residence of a Roman governor

in the Flavian period (AD69–98). However, almost no evidence survives to link the villa with specific individuals. A substantial villa was built on the site under Nero (AD54–68) with baths, colonnaded garden and mosaic-decorated rooms. These were all luxuries then unique in Britain. Ten years later this was demolished to make way for a truly palatial complex.

Visitors approached from the east through a grand porticoed entrance hall that led into landscaped gardens. The main official buildings lay to the west, with an apsed audience hall for the king/governor. The residential wing lay to the north. The palace interior was richly decorated with mosaics in the black-and-white style of the time, with fine marble and stucco-work on the walls. In the 2nd century further buildings, including a bath house, were added, but in AD296 Fishbourne was abandoned after a fire.

Most villas in Britain in the century after the conquests of AD43–84 remained simple. When Tacitus wrote that his father-in-law Agricola, Britain's most far-sighted governor (*c.* AD77–84), persuaded British nobles to build themselves Roman houses, he meant town houses, northern versions of the *domus*. Rural villas developed slowly, sometimes on top of round Iron Age farmsteads – perhaps owned by important Britons Romanizing themselves in the Agricolan way – into rectangular houses of several rooms fronted by a veranda. These corridor villas were often built of timber, which was then abundant in the British Isles. However, the small, late 1st century Villa of Quinton in Northamptonshire was of rectilinear stone built over a round house. At Brixworth nearby, the villa's development can be traced from Celtic round house through successive stages of Roman construction. These developed from the first rectangular house, built AD70–100, which boasted

painted walls, to the grandest 4th-century phase, when a bath house was added. However, the villa remained haphazard in design throughout and was built for use rather than for ostentation.

More impressive is Lullingstone Villa in Kent beside the River Darenth. It was first built (AD 80–90) on a terrace cut into the hill on the winged-corridor pattern. In the 2nd century AD, the "deep room" in the centre, once a grain store, was seemingly turned into a shrine, complete with a painting of nymphs adorning a niche and two fine portrait busts. In the 4th century AD, the central room was reconstructed, with an apse and a mausoleum built to the north. A Christian chapel seems to have been built in one chamber, judging by wall paintings bearing the chi-ro Christian symbol, making the villa one of the few Christian sites in Roman Britain. The villa was burnt down and abandoned early in the 5th century AD.

A GOLDEN AGE

In AD 306, Constantius Chlorus, Augustus (senior emperor) of the West, died in York. He had just returned from a northern campaign that, while only half successful, had restored Roman prestige throughout an island which a decade before had appeared to be slipping out of the Roman orbit under rebel rulers. The half century that followed has been called the golden age of British villas. While towns built themselves ever thicker walls against possible barbarian attacks, villas in southern Britain expanded to sometimes majestic size, apparently unworried by Saxon raiders. Some fertile areas, such as the Fens, have few villas, indicating probably huge imperial estates that precluded private ownership.

Woodchester Villa in Gloucestershire exemplifies the building of the golden age. Started c. AD 100 with a line of buildings on the north side of what became the central courtyard, it was extended southwards around this court in the next 150 years. The villa reached its climax after AD 300 with a grand second northern courtyard

and bath houses. It is famed for its Orpheus mosaic. At 2,500sq ft (225sq m) this was the largest and most ornate mosaic in Britain, showing the mythical Greek poet charming the beasts. Other rooms in this and comparable villas were similarly decorated.

Chedworth Villa in a secluded valley near Cirencester was among Roman Britain's finest. Started in the late 2nd century AD as two houses with a bath suite, it developed in the 3rd and 4th centuries into a single building with two parallel wings connected by a veranda. The north range had elaborate bath suites, beyond which was a small temple with an octagonal pool, possibly devoted to the healing god Lenus-Mars (the Romans assimilated local deities whenever they could). Another villa which was occupied over many centuries is Gadebridge Park, Hertfordshire. Originally built of wood c. AD 100, it grew into a large house of the winged-corridor type in the 4th century. It had a bath suite with a sizeable swimming pool and towers at either end. It was demolished c. AD 350. No Roman villa long survived the collapse of Roman power after AD 400.

Above: Mosaic at Lullingstone Villa, early 4th century AD, showing the Rape of Europa.

Below: Among the greatest Romano-British villas was that at Chedworth in Gloucestershire.

CITIES OF THE EMPIRE

Rome's empire has been called a "confederation of cities". City to the Romans meant a self-governing polity, with its own *curia* (council) of annually elected magistrates. There were more than 1,000 such cities in the empire by AD200, ranging from metropoli such as Carthage to tiny but proud Gloucester. Some were former city-states of great antiquity like Ephesus, prospering again in the long Roman peace. Other cities, especially in the unurbanized West, were new foundations. Trier in Germany, Paris, Nîmes and Arles in France, London and Bath in Britain are cities founded by Romans and still flourishing. Other cities, such as Timgad in North Africa, blossomed and died with the empire, leaving only ruins as eloquent reminders of former wealth. Corinth and Carthage were refounded to boom under the empire after being deleted under the Republic.

As the empire grew, so did its cities, many building theatres, amphitheatres, baths, basilicas and fora, in expensive competition. At times older local traditions – Punic (African), Syrian, Celtic – influenced the classic Graeco-Roman mould. A few cities were seen as emulating Rome: Carthage was called Rome-in-Africa by its inhabitants, and Trier the Rome-of-the-North. Any survey of the empire's cities must start with the two that suffered the singular fate of being preserved for posterity by the eruption of Vesuvius: Pompeii and Herculaneum.

Left: Aerial view of the ruins of Pompeii with Vesuvius in the background, the volcano that both destroyed the city in its eruption of AD79 and preserved it in ash.

POMPEII AND HERCULANEUM

Above: A view of the atrium of the House of the Faun, Pompeii, a typical atrium-style house of a wealthy citizen just before the eruption of AD79 that has so well preserved it.

Below: A map of Pompeii just before the eruption of AD79, showing the major public buildings and the mainly rectilinear street plan. The grey areas on the map are as yet unexcavated.

The eruption that began about midday on 24 August AD79 was a catastrophe for the people of the small cities who had lived for centuries in the fertile lands under Mount Vesuvius – a mountain no one had ever suspected of being a potential volcano. That vast eruption blew the top off the mountain and killed thousands of people. Not realizing their danger, many had remained in the city until too late, although others escaped. The eruption covered Pompeii in 17ft (5m) of volcanic matter and Herculaneum in very hot ash, dust and stones to a depth of up to 70ft (21m), which hardened to form an excellent preservative.

Much of central Italy was powdered in dust, prompting the ever-generous emperor Titus in Rome to promise all the aid he could. It proved of little use and the cities were never reoccupied. They were forgotten until chance discoveries fuelled passionate if destructive excavations from 1748 on. However, Vesuvius' eruption has proved an immense blessing to posterity, for it has preserved – almost ghoulishly – intact the houses, artefacts and corpses of two prosperous, fashionable towns as the Roman empire neared its zenith. Bread has been left preserved in ovens, meals left ready on tables, scurrilous election

notices for the forthcoming *curia* (council) elections – "Thieves support Vatius for aedile!" – survive on the walls. Inside the houses the bodies of lovers have been found entwined in doomed embrace, while in the streets looters were overwhelmed with their booty. Without that terrible day, our knowledge of ordinary Roman life would be far less vivid.

LIFE BEFORE THE ERUPTION

Pompeii was a city long before it came under Roman rule. First inhabited in the 8th century BC, by 500BC it had acquired solid walls made of local tufa and limestone which ran for 2 miles (3.2km). The urban area of some 165 acres (66ha) was not built over completely at first, for there are signs of orchards or gardens within the walls, but by AD79 Pompeii's population was approaching an estimated 15,000. Greek and Etruscan influences, along with the local Samnites', are apparent in the early city. (In the 6th century BC a temple to Apollo, the archetypally Greek deity, was built, but Etruscans also worshipped Apollo.) By the 3rd century BC, Pompeii was under Roman control but Hellenistic influences still predominated artistically, as is most evident in the city's wall paintings.

In 80BC, the dictator Sulla settled about 5,000 Roman veterans with their families in Pompeii, renaming it Colonia Cornelia Veneria Pompeianorum. Local inhabitants must have been displaced but many important public buildings date from soon after this date. However, a major earthquake struck the city in AD62 and at the time of the eruption in AD79, many of the city's buildings were being rebuilt.

In the last century before its end, the Forum acquired notable temples to most Roman gods, indicating that Pompeii was an official religious centre.

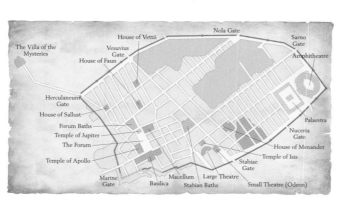

Below: A street crossing showing the stepping stones in what is now called the Via dell'Abbondanza in Pompeii. The city, if small, had all the amenities of a Roman city, including proper paved streets.

THE TEMPLES OF POMPEII

Approaching from the seaward side, the first temple the visitor saw before entering the Forum would have been the Temple of Venus – the divine mother of Aeneas and so, according to later imperial propaganda, of the Julian dynasty. This rose impressively on the right and was probably built by Sulla's colonists. Typically Italian in form, the temple stood inside a wide precinct on a tall platform with a deep colonnaded front porch.

The Temple of Apollo dates to the 6th century BC and, with the Temple on the Triangular Forum, is the oldest building in Pompeii. It stood on the west side of the Forum at a slight angle, suggesting it was planned to align with an earlier Forum. It was much expanded and decorated under Augustus.

The Temple of Jupiter or the Capitolinum was the grandest of Pompeii's temples, in whose ruins a colossal torso of a seated male figure, presumably the king of the gods, has been found. A temple to the recently deified emperor Vespasian (AD69–79), with a wide colonnaded porch, was under construction on the east of the Forum, while next to it the Lararium, a temple to the Lares, the city's guardian gods and intended to ward off further catastrophes, had just been completed. Another temple, that of Isis, had also been swiftly restored. Built originally *c.* 120BC and dedicated to the popular Egyptian goddess – if one whose cult had been half-Hellenized – this had elaborate exterior stucco decorations covering plain brick walls. Interestingly, its restoration was paid for by Numerius Popidius Celsinus, the son of a freedman (former slave), indicating that upward mobility was not uncommon.

Other buildings in the centre added in the city's last century include the vegetable market, the *macellum*, the meat and fish market, and the vast Eumachia, the guild headquarters of the cloth fullers, named after their rich patroness. A large basilica, built 130–120BC – before the city became a Roman colony – had three aisles and fine Ionic columns. The Forum itself was in the process of being rebuilt more grandly with paving in travertine stone when the volcano woke.

Above: The fine Ionic columns of the city's large basilica, built 130–120BC, before Pompeii became a Roman colony.

Below: Fresco still life of a rabbit and figs from the House of the Stags, Herculaneum.

BATHS, THEATRES, AMPHITHEATRES

Pompeii, though it was only a modest provincial city, had public baths and a stone theatre and amphitheatre well before Rome. It boasted five different public bath houses. The largest, the Stabian Baths, dates back to the 4th century BC and came to cover an area of 40,000sq ft (4,000sq m). It is possible that later the Romans were inspired to build public baths with three rooms at progressively higher temperatures by Pompeian examples.

The Pompeians made extensive use of brick from Augustus' time, notably in the façade of the Central Baths, where half-columns alternate with large windows. A big theatre, built partly in stone and more Greek than Roman in plan, predates Rome's first permanent Theatre of Pompey of 55BC by a century.

Pompeii also had one of the first stone amphitheatres (earlier arenas were wooden). Built in the south-east corner of the city against the city walls, which reduced the need for massive earth banks to support its tiers, it probably catered initially for Sulla's veterans. An inscription dates it to about 70BC. With an estimated capacity of 20,000 spectators, it drew crowds from the surrounding area, sometimes with unpredictable consequences. In AD59, an argument over one gladiator led to a full-scale riot between the citizens of Pompeii and those of neighbouring Nuceria, anticipating more recent problems with football hooligans by almost two millennia. The Roman authorities reacted strongly, however, and the Pompeians were banned from holding any further gladiatorial events for ten years.

VILLAS AND HOUSES

Pompeii is famed for its houses which, if not the largest in the empire, are now among the most interesting because they survive in such quantity. Their design shows increasingly strong Hellenistic influences, revealing the city's links to the Greek East.

Early houses like the House of the Surgeon, built before 200BC, which centred round the *atrium*, gave way to more luxurious houses in which the *peristyle* and gardens gained ever greater importance. The House of the Gilded Cupids, built c. 150BC, had a huge *peristyle*, which was effectively a colonnaded garden. The House of the Faun, among the largest in Pompeii, covers about 1 acre (0.4 ha). Decorated throughout in the elegant, rather austere First Style, it progresses from an entrance passage through the *atrium* with bedrooms only on the left, to another bigger *atrium* opening to the right, which has two Ionic columns of tufa. Beyond this lies the room which contains the Alexander the Great mosaic. Perhaps the most famous mosaic in Pompeii, it was copied from a Greek painting. Beyond lies a large garden.

Increasingly, wealthier citizens tended to move out of town. About 400 yards out of Pompeii stands the famous Villa of the Mysteries. Built on an artificial earth platform, it is entered by the *peristyle*. Beyond this is a large *atrium* on the far side of which is a *tablinium* (central room) overlooking the sea. The house, which dates from the 2nd century BC with later alterations, is vast; it has 60 rooms and covers 1.4 acres (0.56 ha). Its famous murals show in dramatic detail scenes of a mystery religion, probably that of the god Dionysus.

A bedroom in a villa at Boscoreale outside Pompeii was decorated with murals showing gardens, fountains and bowls of fruits in frescoes. The murals are expressive of the superb illusionistic skills of the Second Style of the mid-1st century BC. Here too the inspiration was Greek.

By AD79, in luxurious houses like that of Loreius Tiburtinus, which was being extended at the time of the eruption, the *peristyle* had shrunk. The still spacious *atrium* was flanked by two-storeyed buildings, but the *peristyle* simply led into the long formal garden on to which many rooms, including the luxurious *triclinium*, opened. With its pergolas, statues and fountains, the garden was clearly the villa's real focus, from which a view of the mountains could be enjoyed.

HERCULANEUM
Smaller and far less extensively excavated than Pompeii, due to the hard, compacted volcanic material, which buried it, and the busy modern town above it, Roman Herculaneum boasts fine villas overlooking the sea. The Bay of Naples was considered to have some of the finest scenery in Italy, as well as the best climate.

Here the *peristyle* was replacing the *atrium*, as is evident in two adjoining villas built on terraces over the city walls, the House of the Stag and the House of the Mosaic Atrium. In the latter, built in the mid-1st century AD, the traditional pattern was partly followed in the north wing. It had an *atrium* minus its side

rooms and then a large central garden surrounded by rooms on two floors with a *triclinium* at the far end. Two small living rooms flanked a long narrow terrace, in the centre of which were the main reception rooms.

In the House of the Stags the *atrium* is only an entrance lobby with rooms arranged symmetrically around the garden courtyard. The inner *triclinium* faces on to this courtyard. Villas such as these had magnificent decorations. These often took the form of vividly realistic murals such as that of the Tragic Actor and show Graeco-Roman painting at its zenith.

Above: This fresco shows the riot in the amphitheatre between the people of Pompeii and those of nearby Nuceria in AD59. The amphitheatre at Pompeii is the earliest dated example of a permanent amphitheatre.

Below: Pompeii's Forum was dominated by the temple that is thought to have been dedicated to Jupiter, king of the gods. In its ruins was found the colossal torso of a seated male figure.

OSTIA AND PORTUS

Above: The ruins of the Baths of the Charioteers, one of 18 such baths in Ostia.

Below: A portico in Ostia decorated c. AD120 in the fashionable black and white style with ships, the symbols of Ostia's then booming trade.

Ostia, situated at the mouth of the Tiber, was one of Rome's first colonies. Founded *c.* 350BC as a base against pirates, its walls covered only five acres (2 ha). Later it became one of the colonies Sulla took for his veterans, expanding its walled area to around 160 acres (64ha). Ostia was early Rome's main port, but its harbour was open to storms and plagued by sandbars, and never ideal because it was a river port and could not cope with big ships. As Rome became crucially dependent on imported grain, Pozzuoli (Puteoli) near Naples became the deep water harbour for Rome. There, goods were transhipped to barges which crawled along the coast to Ostia. The latter was still Rome's outlet to the sea. This was expensive and risky, so in AD42 Claudius, reviving one of Julius Caesar's grand projects, decided to build an artificial harbour on the coast two miles north of Ostia, called Portus.

THE BUILDING OF PORTUS

A gigantic ship with a displacement of 7,400 tons, used by Caligula to transport an obelisk from Egypt, was sunk to provide the base for a large *pharos* (lighthouse). Breakwaters were built to make a harbour 1,200yds (1,100m) across., but storms still wrecked ships sheltering inside the wide harbour – Tacitus records 200 sunk in AD62 alone – and most grain fleets still avoided Ostia in favour of Pozzuoli.

Trajan (ruled AD98–117) solved the problem by excavating an octagonal inner basin about 770yds (700m) across, with a canal link to the Tiber. Flanked by large warehouses, the new quays at Portus had numbered columns corresponding to mooring berths. More than 100 ships could dock in its inner basin at the same time, while the outer harbour was used as a holding area for arriving ships.

Ostia boomed thanks to Portus' new dock and for two centuries the places' fortunes intertwined. Many merchants, chandlers and others associated with Rome's import trade – Rome *exported* nothing except edicts, administrators and refuse – lived in Ostia, although they presumably worked in Portus. Their joint population approached an estimated 100,000 at their 2nd-century peak.

Ostia declined in the 4th century and its buildings were abandoned to the river silt that finally blocked up its harbour. The river silt also, however, preserved Ostia's buildings, to provide evidence of how ordinary Romans lived.

Private houses initially remained mostly simple *domus* (individual house) types, some half-timbered, although they began to unite their porticoes to create colonnades

like those of Eastern cities. The rebuilding of Ostia began under Domitian, and, with Trajan's new docks, Ostia was rapidly transformed into a showcase of contemporary Roman building techniques.

REBUILDING OSTIA

The western quarter was rebuilt first with *insulae* (apartment blocks) in brick-faced concrete. Although not covered in stucco, this was meant to be seen, as arched doorways and balconies broke up its otherwise plain façades. The *insulae* rivalled those of the capital but at a lower density – they seldom rose more than four floors – and are today much better preserved.

The House of Diana is a typical *insula*. Its south and west sides had large windows facing the street but the other sides, which adjoined neighbouring houses, lacked windows. To give them light, the architect put a courtyard in the centre, along with a water cistern for all residents to use, as piped water was a luxury restricted to the first floor at best.

Fronting the streets were *tabernae* – single-roomed shops with a mezzanine above where the shopkeepers often lived. Staircases between the shops led to the upper floors. Many *insulae* looked impressive and some, with inner gardens, were spacious and comfortable.

Even the city's warehouses were imposingly built. The Horra Epagathiania of *c.* AD150 had an arched entrance made of brick but flanked by proper Corinthian columns with pediments.

Among the major public buildings was the Capitolium (Temple to Jupiter, Juno and Minerva). Built on the Forum's north side *c.* AD120–30, it stood at the end of a broad street which led down to the river and was flanked by brick porticoes. Built of brick-faced concrete sumptuously covered in marble, it was raised on a high podium to dominate surrounding buildings and measured about 70ft (22m) tall. A temple to Roma and Augustus, also covered in marble, dates from Tiberius' reign (AD14–37), but Ostia's many temples to more exotic gods reveal foreign influences. The city also had at least 18 public baths, reflecting Roman priorities. Of these, the Forum Baths (*c.* AD150) is the finest, its octagonal west-facing room recalling the sun rooms in Hadrian's Villa at Tivoli.

This surge of building activity faded after AD160. In the 4th century AD, as Ostia's population fell to make more space available for bigger houses, some fine new *domus* were built, such as the House of Cupid and Psyche.

By the 4th century AD Ostia was in decline as Portus supplanted it. Although far smaller, Portus had notable buildings of its own, including the Imperial Palace, which lay on the western quay of the new basin looking out over Claudius' harbour. Built of fine brick-faced concrete with a bath house, it was probably connected with the administration or it may have been the Forum. Portus was to remain Rome's port for centuries.

Above: Ships laden with amphorae (earthenware jars) sailing past the lighthouse at Ostia. This 3rd-century AD relief is rather unusual as it comes from a Christian tomb in the Catacombs of Praetextatus.

Below: The House of Diana in Ostia. A typical insula *(apartment block), with large windows facing the street and a light-well and courtyard behind it, it dates from the early 2nd century AD.*

CONTRASTING CITIES: CARTHAGE AND TIMGAD

Above: Corinthian capitals of the Antonine Baths, Carthage.

Below: Ruins of the Punic district of ancient Carthage.

Founded by the Phoenicians in 814BC, Carthage swiftly became the most powerful city in the western Mediterranean, with an extensive commercial network, and later Rome's most feared opponent. Hannibal, its great general, devastated Italy in the Second Punic War (218–202BC) and even threatened Rome itself, so Carthage's total destruction by Rome in 146BC was an act of delayed revenge. Yet Carthage's superb site, with fine harbours and fertile hinterland, led Romans such as the reformer Gaius Gracchus in 122BC and later Julius Caesar to propose a colony there. Under Augustus, these plans were realized in 29BC with the foundation of Colonia Julia Concordia Karthago. Three thousand colonists were settled on what became one of the empire's largest cities and the magnificent capital of one of Rome's richest provinces.

ROMAN MEETS PUNIC CULTURE

If the Romans had tried to delete all traces of the Punic city in 146BC, the suburbs of modern Tunis today cover the Roman city very effectively. However, enough has been excavated to show that Augustus' surveyors created a typical grid pattern for the new city.

The old Punic citadel of Byrsa was levelled to make a rectangular platform of about 10 acres (4ha) on which the usual public buildings – forum, basilica, temples – were erected. Local topography meant, however, that the Roman city followed the general alignment of its Punic predecessor, while its inhabitants themselves became a mixture of Roman newcomers and slowly Romanized Punic inhabitants. An altar to the *gens Augusta* (family of Augustus) deliberately recalled the Ara Pacis (Altar of Peace) in Rome. The Capitoline triad was worshipped but local Punic gods were also tolerated and assimilated into the Roman pantheon. Only Moloch with his reputation for human sacrifice was excluded.

Punic Carthage had been renowned for its rectangular outer harbour and an inner, circular harbour reputedly able to shelter and launch 200 galleys. Carthage now became the chief port as well as capital of the Roman province of Africa. As the province became Rome's main source of wheat and olive oil, the harbours were rebuilt for more peaceful traffic. A large amphitheatre was built in the west of the city around the time of Augustus, along with a circus 1,700ft (516m) long, able to seat up to 55,000 people. Only the Circus Maximus in Rome itself was larger. Under Hadrian (ruled AD117–38) a luxurious theatre, decorated in marble, onyx, granite and porphyry, was constructed. Finally, the immense Antonine Baths were built in AD143–62, the largest baths outside Rome itself at the time. With an ingeniously planned ring of interlocking hexagonal *caldaria* (hot baths), these were enormous – 650ft (200m) long, covering 192,000sq ft (17,850sq m) – and richly decorated with mosaics and imported marbles. An aqueduct, substantial parts of which survive, brought water from 35 miles (56km) away, supplying an estimated 7 million gallons (32 million litres) a day to the city.

From Carthage came Apuleius, the novelist of the 2nd century AD and a short-lived dynasty of emperors, the Gordiani (AD238–4). St Augustine, the great theologian, lived there AD370–83 (Carthage was an important centre of early Christianity) and praised its tree-lined avenues and many churches. Despite conquest by the Vandals in the 5th century, the city remained a bastion of Roman culture and provided loyal support to the Byzantine empire after it was restored to the empire in AD535. Carthage only fell to Arab invaders after prolonged sieges in AD698, a fall that marked the end, after seven centuries, of Rome in Africa.

TIMGAD: A VETERANS' COLONY

Almost 200 miles (320km) south-west of Carthage, on a low and then fertile plateau, stand the ruins of a very different city, Timgad (Thamugadi) in modern Algeria. Founded by Trajan in AD100 as a colony for veterans, it was planned exactly like a large legionary camp, forming a square of 1,200 Roman feet (1,165 ft/355m) subdivided into 12 equal blocks, each 100 Roman feet square. The two main streets – the *cardo* and *decumanus* – intersect at the exact centre, where lay the forum with a basilica,

a *curia* (local senate house), temple and public lavatory – this last a building of some elegance, with marble arm rests in the shape of dolphins. Just to the north was the 4,000-seat theatre.

Intended to provide homes for retired legionaries and to help Romanize a still half-wild region, Timgad grew into a town with a population of around 15,000 people by AD200. It spread rather chaotically beyond its original plan as more baths, temples and a library were built. At first its houses were simple if solid single-storey buildings made of local limestone and timber – the mountains nearby were then well wooded – but with continuous colonnades in the Eastern style.

Before the city of Timgad was totally abandoned in the 7th century AD, a small Byzantine fort was built to the south. Most spectacular of the surviving ruins is the triple Arch of Trajan – which was actually built *c.* AD190, and so commemorates the city's famous founder – with pediments above the side arches, at the end of a colonnaded street.

Above: A servant offering a diner wine in a mosaic from Carthage of the early 4th century AD. Carthage soon became second only to Rome in the Western empire in its size and wealth.

Below: The triple Arch of Trajan standing at the end of a colonnaded street in Timgad. It was built about AD190 to commemorate the city's imperial founder.

LEPCIS MAGNA: AN EMPEROR'S BIRTHPLACE

Above: A bust of Septimius Severus (AD146–211), Lepcis's most famous son who became emperor in AD193 and richly adorned the city.

Below: One of the central pavilions of the macellum (market) in Lepcis. It was built c. 8BC of the fine local limestone as the city grew under the Augustan peace.

Lepcis Magna in Tripolitania (western Libya) was founded by the Phoenicians or Carthaginians c. 600BC. A Punic (Carthaginian) city long before it became part of the Roman empire after 100BC, under the Pax Augusta, the 250-year-long peace established by Augustus in 30BC, it became steadily more prosperous. It was opulently adorned by its greatest native son Septimius Severus, emperor AD193–211. Later totally abandoned, its surviving ruins are among the finest of any Roman city.

Little remains of pre-Roman Lepcis, although many of its inhabitants long spoke Punic as well as Latin. Under Augustus, the Old Forum by the sea was laid out on standard rectangular lines, except in the north-east where an earlier temple survived. The three new temples are typically Italian in style, with high podiums and frontal emphasis. The central temple to the goddess Roma and Augustus was dedicated c. AD18. A *macellum* (market) with two central octagonal pavilions was built inside a rectangular courtyard in 8BC, with shops sheltering from the harsh African sun under its porticoes. A private citizen, Annobal Rufus built the theatre in AD1–2, which had an auditorium 300ft (90m) across. Partly resting on a natural slope, it had a splendid *scaenae frons* (stage wall), with three tiers of curving columns (some later rebuilt in marble) and a slot in the floor into which the curtain was lowered before performances.

GROWING PROSPERITY

Under Hadrian, magnificent new baths modelled on those of Trajan in Rome were erected in AD126–7. They made novel use of expensive marbles that were imported from Greece or Asia Minor even in their well-appointed communal lavatories, which could seat 60 people. The baths had the usual *natatio* (swimming pool), *tepidarium* (warm room) and *caldarium* (hot room) sequence, with the addition of *sudatoria* (sweat rooms), ancestors of the Turkish bath. They reveal Lepcis Magna's growing prosperity, as careful dry farming techniques, capturing and conserving every drop of rain, pushed back the desert to give Tripolitania its golden age.

Many public buildings were now opulently remodelled in marble. The Hunting Baths, externally unadorned concrete vaulted structures on the beach, are notable architecturally. They may have been used by wealthy local huntsmen, but the name comes from the hunting scenes painted on the vaults inside. It is thought they might have served as the baths of a guild or as private baths which could be hired by groups. By the 2nd century AD, Lepcis was one of the empire's richest cities, but its best was yet to come.

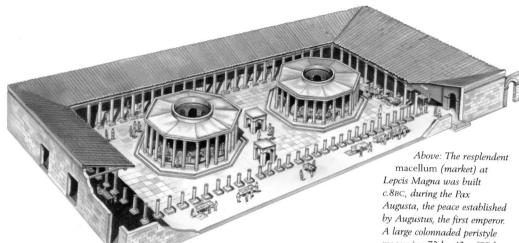

SEVERAN HEYDAY

Septimius Severus was a senator (of Rome) and commander of the Danubian legions when he launched his bid for the imperial throne in AD193, but he always remained faithful to his home town. Indeed, his family was so obviously Libyan that it is reported that he had to send his sister back home because her marked Lepcis accent made her ridiculous at court. Septimius endowed his native city with a new monumental quarter, including an enclosed harbour, temple, new forum and basilica and a piazza dominated by a huge *nymphaeum* (fountain building) – buildings that would have looked impressive even in Rome.

The harbour was a circular basin about 400yds (365m) in diameter with a lighthouse and warehouses. From the waterfront a colonnaded street about 450yds (411m) long and 70ft (21m) wide, flanked by porticoes, led up to the piazza near the Hadrianic baths. North of this Severus built a new forum, 200 by 330ft (60 by 100m).

On the forum's south-west side was a vast temple to the Severan family. Standing on a double-height podium on a tall flight of steps, it had eight red Egyptian granite columns in front, with columns of green *cipollino* marble with white Pentelic marble capitals on either side. It resembled but surpassed in grandeur Augustus' Temple of Mars Ultor in Rome. On the other side of the forum rose a huge new basilica, over 100ft (30m) high, with apses at both ends flanked by two pairs of white marble pilasters. The galleries over the double height lateral aisles were supported by Corinthian columns of red Egyptian granite. The timber roof had a span of 62ft (19m). Elaborate coloured marbles were used throughout Severus' projects. The raw materials and the craftsmen were imported; even the unknown architect probably came from the Aegean world.

The Forum was surrounded by a high masonry wall – it became a fortress under the Byzantines – but inside ran an opulent arcaded portico with alternating Medusa and Nereid heads. The *nymphaeum* had a big semicircular fountain basin, which was richly decorated with niches and columns of red granite.

In gratitude for this imperial largesse, the citizens of Lepcis erected a triumphal arch to their emperor for his visit in AD203. Four-sided, it has exuberant decorations, with columns, winged Victories holding wreaths and reliefs showing Severus and his triumphant armies. Lepcis was finally covered by sand as the collapse of Roman farming methods allowed the Sahara to push north to the coast.

Above: The resplendent macellum (market) at Lepcis Magna was built c.8BC, during the Pax Augusta, the peace established by Augustus, the first emperor. A large colonnaded peristyle measuring 73 by 43m (80 by 47yds) surrounds the macellum. Two circular market-halls, rather than the usual single hall, stood in the centre, crowded with market stalls. Its size shows Lepcis was already a wealthy city.

Below: The citizens of Lepcis erected a four-sided triumphal arch in gratitude to their emperor Severus for his visit in AD203. It was exuberantly decorated with winged victories holding wreaths.

ATHENS: A GLORIOUS PAST

Above: Tiers of marble seats in the Theatre of Dionysus in Athens, refurbished and restored under the Romans.

Below: The School of Plato, traditionally the greatest of Greek philosophers, shown in a 1st century AD mosaic.

Athens lost its last political importance after Sulla brutally sacked it in 86BC for supporting Mithradates' war against Rome. However, it retained a unique status in the empire broadly comparable to that of Florence or Venice today, under which it was revered for its past artistic and intellectual glories. Illustrious Romans, from the great orator Cicero in 80BC to the last pagan emperor Julian in AD354, studied in Athens, while emperors endowed it with new buildings or special privileges. Far smaller than Hellenistic cities such as Alexandria, Athens was still recognized as the cultural capital of Greece and its craftsmen's skills were much appreciated in Rome. It even regained its position as the chief centre of philosophy. It did not, however, regain its democracy, for emperors were also making

a political point through their buildings, emphasizing Rome's power over Greece. Roman imperial monuments filled up the old *agora* (forum), which had once been the centre of Athenian democratic life. Most Athenians, who had suffered in Rome's civil wars, were too impoverished to object to the wealthy new masters who gave them work.

PROCLAIMING ROMAN POWER

Julius Caesar had provided money for a new *agora* that was built under Augustus and dedicated in 10BC. A rectangular court 270 by 225ft (82 by 69m), it was enclosed by Ionic porticoes and entered by a monumental gateway whose style revived Athenian 5th-century BC classicism. (Augustus chiefly admired Greek classicism for its air of dignity and authority.) Greek cities in the East used brick, stone and mortared rubble rather than Roman concrete. The Temple of Ares (Mars), originally 5th century BC and erected elsewhere in Attica, was moved block by block into the Agora and linked with Augustus' temple of Mars Ultor in Rome.

In 15BC Agrippa, Augustus' chief minister, built an *odeion* (roofed theatre), a lofty rectangular gabled hall to seat about 1,000. Its carved marble ornaments again copied classical examples but its giant scale – its interior was 76ft (23m) high and 82ft (25m) square – was new in Athens. A small circular temple to Rome and Augustus was built on the Acropolis. This was artistically influenced by the nearby classical Erechtheion but politically it proclaimed the power of Rome.

The flamboyantly philhellenic emperor Nero refurbished the old Theatre of Dionysus beneath the Acropolis between AD54 and 61, erecting a Roman-style stage building. This had seen the first performances of most of the great Greek tragedies by Aeschylus, Sophocles and

Euripides. It now also witnessed gladiatorial games. The games themselves
apparently became popular with some
Athenians after an initial period of
disgust. Meanwhile, wealthy young
Romans came to Athens to study at one
of the competing schools of philosophy:
Stoic, Platonist, Epicurean or Cynic.

THE CITY OF HADRIAN

By the early 2nd century AD, Athens had
regained a modest prosperity through the
export of its fine Pentelic marble and
skilled craftsmen. The emperor Hadrian,
whose philhellenism ran deep, spent some
of his happiest years in the city he first
visited in AD124–5.

Hadrian became *archon* (mayor) of
Athens and made the city head of his new
Panhellenion League (an essentially
honorific title). He also completed the
temple of Olympian Zeus (Jupiter) whose
building was started by the tyrant Peisistratus
in the 6th century BC and revived in 174BC
by the Seleucid king Antiochus IV.
Antiochus' Roman architects, the Cossutius
brothers, had opted for the Corinthian
order for the 60ft (18m) high columns,
but the huge temple had suffered when
Sulla removed many columns to Rome.
Hadrian dedicated it in AD132, placing a
chryselephantine (gold and ivory) statue
of Zeus inside the building.

Hadrian also provided a new aqueduct,
a library whose plan recalled the Forum
Pacis in Rome, a *stoa* (portico) with
symmetrical gardens and baths. To
commemorate his work, Hadrian erected
an arch at the boundary between the
original city and the new quarter he had
founded in AD131. This was not in the
usual triumphant Roman style but linked
him to Theseus, Athens' legendary
founder. The inscriptions on one side read,
"This is the city of Theseus, not Hadrian",
and on the other, "This is the city of
Hadrian, not Theseus".

In AD143, Herodes Atticus, a wealthy
aristocrat, restored the Hellenistic stadium
(which was used for the Panathenaic
games) in Pentelic marble. The stadium

was also used for gladiatorial games after
this restoration. He built a new marble
odeion, but there was little further
construction. Third-century troubles saw
Athens sacked in AD256 by marauding
barbarians and, like so many cities at this
time, it rewalled itself. More damagingly,
the Visigoths under Alaric ravaged all
Greece in AD398, attacking pagan temples
in particular. (The Visigoths were keen,
if heretical, Christians, but the remaining
temple treasures were the chief attraction.)
Despite this, Plato's Academy continued
to flourish as the centre of Neoplatonism,
the last great philosophical movement of
antiquity. Proclus (*c.* AD410–85), who
lectured in Athens, was its supreme
systematizer. He extended the thinking
of its founder, Plotinus, to stress the
interconnectedness of all things, arguing
that time itself is a circular dance.

However, Christian intolerance was
growing. In AD529 the Byzantine emperor
Justinian ordered the closure of all
the schools of philosophy, so ending a
thousand years of intellectual freedom
and ancient Athens itself.

*Above: The gigantic Temple of
Olympian Zeus was
completed by Hadrian in
AD132, some 650 years after
it was started.*

*Below: The Tower of the
Winds, which housed an
elaborate monumental clock
dating from c. 50BC.*

TRIER: THE ROME OF THE NORTH

Above: The now plain interior of the huge Basilica was once decorated with glowing mosaics that surrounded the emperor enthroned in majesty in the apse at the far end.

Below: The Porta Nigra (Black Gate), the northern gateway, rises 100ft (30m) and dates from c. AD300. Its unusually fine state of preservation is due to its conversion into a chapel in the Middle Ages.

Three days' march up the Moselle valley from the Rhine frontier, Trier (Augusta Treverorum) had a superb strategic position. When Postumus proclaimed his separatist Gallic empire in AD260, he made Trier his capital, but in the ensuing civil war and invasions the city was sacked. It recovered, however, to become the leading city in the Western empire in the 4th century AD. Politically, economically and culturally it supplanted Lyons (Lugdunum), which never recovered from being sacked by Septimius Severus in the civil wars of AD195.

ORIGINS OF A CITY

There was no pre-Roman settlement at Trier when Agrippa, Augustus' general, chose the site for a military camp. This attracted the local Celts and a township grew up around it. (The Treveri had been a warlike people, supplying Caesar with cavalry, but had not previously been city dwellers.) Under Claudius (ruled AD43–54) Trier gained the important status of *colonia* and a charter. It developed rapidly thanks to its position on the major trade routes

that ran north–south and east–west and to the stone bridge which Claudius had constructed. Its piers still support the modern bridge. Trier became the seat of the procurator (governor) of the province of Gallia Belgica. There are traces of houses with stone foundations and a large rectangular hall from the 1st century AD.

Soon after AD100, the grand St Barbara Baths were constructed. Elaborately decorated, with marble statues in semicircular niches around an open-air *natatio* (swimming pool), they also had several heated rooms, essential in a city so far north. Along with a stone amphitheatre that could seat up to 20,000 people, private houses were now constructed that boasted fine mosaic floors. The Forum, about 1,300 by 500ft (400 by 150m), was built around this time, as was the *curia* (council room). The monumental northern gateway known as the Porta Nigra (Black Gate – age has weathered it) is an early 4th-century building in a deliberately archaic style. At 100ft (30m) high and 120ft (36m) long, it was intended to impress visitors or invaders with the majesty of Rome, with its many tiered arches flanked by pillars. It may have been left unfinished, which accounts for the rough, even crude quality of its stonework. Its survival is due to its conversion into a chapel in the Middle Ages.

A GOLDEN AGE

In AD293 Constantius Chlorus became Caesar (junior emperor) of the West from Morocco to the Tyne, and Augustus (senior emperor) in AD305. Like the other tetrarchs, he chose a permanent new capital, in his case Trier, and adorned it lavishly. Among his new structures was the Basilica, although it was probably completed by his son Constantine I who held court at Trier from AD306–312. Built of solid red brick, the Basilica is a huge

bare hall, measuring around 95 by 220ft (29 by 67m) and almost 100ft (30m) high. Part of the imperial palace, it was not then a free-standing building. Today it is a completely plain Lutheran church, lit by two rows of round-headed windows, which continue around the apse. The upper windows of the apse are lower and shorter than those in the nave, producing the illusion that the apse is larger than it is. This effect was intended to magnify the power of the emperor who sat enthroned in its mosaic-covered apse. The floor was originally covered in black and white marble and heated by hypocausts, which were themselves veneered in marble. The exterior of the building would not originally have seemed as austere as it does now, because it was probably stuccoed and had two rows of wooden balconies around it.

Equally imposing buildings formed the Kaiserthermen (Imperial Baths) erected after AD293 at the southern end of the palace complex, probably for courtiers' sole use. Their main bathing-block (450 by 400ft/ 137 by 122m) occupied half the rectangular site, facing the large porticoed court and surrounding buildings. They may not have been completed when Constantine finally left Trier in AD316, and only parts were used as baths by later emperors. Other parts were probably used as offices.

A CENTRE OF CULTURE

Trier continued to enjoy imperial favour. Constantine II and later Valentinian I (AD364–75) and his son Gratian (AD375–83) all chose to rule from it. Constantine I had started its polygonal cathedral, the first in northern Europe, which now forms part of Trier Cathedral.

Two massive limestone warehouses were built near the river, each 230ft long by 65ft wide (70 by 120m). About AD300 city walls, 20ft high and 10ft thick (6m by 3m), with 75 towers, were built to enclose an area of 700 acres (280ha).

In the 4th century AD, Trier was a centre of culture as well as power, with its own university. Ausonius, the poet and courtier who tutored the young Gratian,

famously praised the beautiful Moselle valley and its terraced vineyards in his poems. Other intellectually distinguished visitors included St Augustine, St Jerome – both key Church fathers – and Lactantius, a noted Christian orator. Trier deserved its title *Roma Transalpina*, Rome north of the Alps, but it did not survive the calamitous 5th century. Finally abandoned by the imperial court in AD395, it was sacked by German invaders in AD406.

Above: A carving on a tombstone of the 2nd century AD showing a tavern scene (top) and a wine barrel being transported by ox cart (beneath). The Moselle valley was already famed for its wines under the Romans.

EPHESUS: WONDER OF THE WORLD

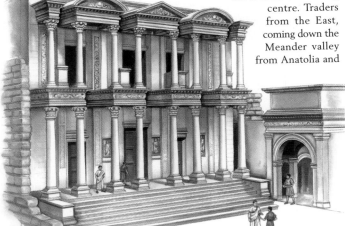

Above: Artemis (Diana), the great goddess of the Ephesians, portrayed as a fertility goddess with many breasts in this statue of the 2nd century AD. Her huge temple was one of the seven wonders of the world.

Ephesus was a very ancient city dating back to Mycenaean times when the Romans made it the capital of their new province of Asia (western Anatolia) in *c.* 129BC. Like Athens, Ephesus had long been an important intellectual and religious as well as commercial centre. However, unlike Athens, it boomed under the Pax Romana, becoming one of the wealthiest cities in the empire, with a population of perhaps 200,000 people. Large areas of the central city have been excavated and many buildings testify to this long prosperity. While remaining firmly Greek in spirit, Ephesus' architecture was more innovative than Athens', reflecting its citizens' greater wealth and self-confidence.

Up to *c.* 180BC, Ephesus had thrived, sometimes as the Western capital of the vast Seleucid empire, more often as an independent city state. However, Rome's wars – especially its civil wars – half-ruined the Greek cities of Asia Minor and Ephesus only recovered after Augustus had restored peace in 30BC. The city grew rich primarily from trade, as it was never a manufacturing centre. Traders from the East, coming down the Meander valley from Anatolia and points east as far as China, which was then the world's only source of silk, offloaded their valuable cargoes in the port at Ephesus on to ships bound for Rome.

DIANA OF THE EPHESIANS

Ephesus' gigantic temple of Artemis (Diana) – traditionally built with money provided by the wealthy King Croesus of Lydia *c.* 550BC and certainly dating to before 500BC – was another, if smaller, source of wealth and a great source of civic pride. It was among the first Greek temples to use the Ionic order throughout, rather than the Doric or Aeolian orders. Many times restored or rebuilt to the same design after fires (one of them started deliberately), the temple was constructed mostly of marble and considered one of the seven wonders of the ancient world, chiefly because of its size. It measured 374ft by 180ft (114 by 55m). With its huge Ionic columns 65ft (20m) high, it was the largest temple of the classic rectilinear column and lintel type ever constructed. Within its *cella* (central chamber) was a giant statue of Artemis, depicted not as the usual chaste huntress-goddess of Graeco-Roman mythology but as a many-breasted deity, pointing to the Asian origin of her cult at Ephesus.

Around the temple precincts swarmed peddlers of locally made religious trinkets. Theirs was the highly profitable trade that St Paul tried to disrupt on his mission, causing local craftsmen to riot shouting, "Great is Diana (Artemis) of the Ephesians!" After Constantine had made Christianity fashionable, however, Ephesus became an important Christian city and the seat of a bishop.

Left: The Library of Celsus, Ephesus, built c. AD110. It is remarkable for its undulating façade with projecting pavilions topped by curved and triangular pediments.

THE ARKADIANE

Ephesus had reasonably abundant building materials and most of its public buildings in the Roman period were of solid masonry. This applied to the colonnaded street, running 650yds (600m) from the harbour to the theatre – superbly sited at the foot of Mount Pion – called the Arkadiane. Along this 36ft (11m) broad avenue lay most of the important buildings of the Roman era.

The Library of Celsus was among the most striking of the buildings of Ephesus. Dating from about AD110–35, it stands at the bottom of Euretes Street. It was built by the son and grandson of a rich and illustrious citizen, Caius Julius Celsus Polemeanus, who had become a consul in Rome – the highest honour a normal citizen could attain – and who was, most unusually, buried inside the Library beneath its apse. A tall rectangular hall, 55ft wide by 36ft long (16.7 by 10.9m), it had a small central apse with a statue of Celsus. Round three sides ran three rows of recesses to house the books or scrolls. Two orders of columns carried the two tiers of balustraded galleries to give access to the upper bookcases. Its richly carved façade has been re-erected, revealing that pairs of upper columns were staggered over the lower columns and alternated with curved and triangular pediments. This has shown that Ephesian architects could play sparkling new variations on old classical themes. The nearby Temple to Hadrian – which was erected by a private citizen and is therefore relatively small – is remarkable for its Syrian arch where the central span of the façade is arched up into the pediment. Like the colonnaded Arkadiane, this may also have been Syrian-inspired.

The most innovatory buildings of Roman Ephesus were its numerous resplendent baths. Largest of these were the Harbour Baths of the late 1st century

Right: The Temple of Hadrian, built AD130–8, has an ornate frieze across its façade rising up into an arch resting on two Corinthian columns.

AD. In the centre of this bulky complex lay the two *Marmorsaalen* (Marble Rooms), opulently decorated marble halls on either side of a *peristyle* court, with the baths themselves in between. The Greek preference for gymnasia with covered running tracks distinguishes these baths from those in the Romanized Western empire. Such very Greek taste for athletics and classical architecture survived until the advent of Christianity in the 4th century.

Above: Detail of a garland from a sarcophagus, probably from the 2nd century AD, when Ephesus was booming under Roman rule. The dynamic exuberance of this relief illustrates the self-confidence and wealth of the city at the time.

VANISHED CITIES OF THE EAST

Above: The Temple of Bel in Palmyra, dedicated in AD32, is Hellenistic in its tall Corinthian columns, but its entrance by a grand side doorway is not at all classical.

Below: Reconstruction of the markedly Graeco-Roman theatre in Palmyra. Here its most famous ruler, Queen Zenobia, reputedly liked to watch Greek dramas after her victories.

Pompey had added western Asia from the Caucasus to the Red Sea to the Roman sphere of influence in the 60s BC, but it was centuries before Rome directly controlled all this area, home of many ancient civilizations. While most cities gained a Hellenistic veneer after Alexander the Great's conquests (334–323BC) – and metropoli like Antioch in Syria or Seleucia-on-the-Tigris were totally new Greek-speaking foundations – the population remained mainly Aramaic-speaking (Semitic). This made for a fertile mixture of styles. Meanwhile, the Pax Romana allowed long-distance trade to flourish even beyond Rome's eastern frontier.

PALMYRA

Located in the Syrian desert, Palmyra, long a semi-independent client state, was well situated to benefit from this peace. The city was an oasis midway between the Euphrates and the Mediterranean ports. Its excellent cavalry – it included heavy armoured cataphracts besides mounted archers – protected caravans carrying the spices and other exotic goods so valued in Rome and it became a major caravan city on the trade routes with the East. (The "protection" may not have been entirely voluntary, but it helped rather than hindered trade.) Visiting Palmyra in AD128, Hadrian granted it the status of "free city", allowing it to set its own taxes and dues. It consequently prospered even more, while moving closer into the Roman orbit. The Palmyrene Tariff is a list of taxes charged for goods coming and going and for the use of the springs.

AN AUDACIOUS QUEEN

When the Persians over-ran Rome's eastern provinces and captured the emperor Valerian in AD260, Odenathus, ruler of Palmyra, rode to Rome's rescue. His cavalry drove the Persians out of Syria and Anatolia and he won himself the title *Dux Orientis* (Duke of the East), before he was assassinated in AD267. His widow Zenobia, noted alike for her dark-haired beauty and for her audacity, inherited his power.

Zenobia claimed descent from Cleopatra, the last Ptolemaic queen of Egypt, and rivalled her in ambition. The great historian Edward Gibbon, admittedly writing 1,500 years later, called her, "The most lovely as well as the most heroic of her sex…Her large black eyes sparkled with an uncommon fire, tempered by the most attractive sweetness".

Proclaiming her son Augustus and herself Augusta, Zenobia rejected Roman suzerainty and invaded Egypt in AD270. Finally provoked, the emperor Aurelian marched east and crushed her in a series of battles, capturing Palmyra in AD271. After these defeats the city became a

Roman frontier fort – an ignominious fate that, paradoxically, has preserved it well. The most striking aspect of Palmyra today is its long colonnaded streets. The main colonnaded street, dating from the early 2nd century AD and three-quarters of a mile (1.2km) long and 35ft (11m) wide, ran from the Grove Temple in the west to the Temple of Bel, intersecting similarly colonnaded streets.

The great temple of Bel, the city's chief deity of Babylonian origin, was dedicated in AD32. From the outside it appears to follow classical canons fairly closely, with six columns at either end on a low platform, like many Hellenistic temples. However, it is far from classical in layout. It is entered not from the front but through an elaborate doorway at the head of a grand staircase on the west side. Inside are two cult chambers. It was possibly topped by a parapet of crowstepped merlons and its roof, behind its classical pediments, had flat terraces. Parthian influences are also apparent in many of its statues, which are stiffly stylized. However, architecturally Palmyra became more Graeco-Roman in the following centuries, with the construction of an *agora* (forum), a theatre – where Zenobia reputedly watched Greek dramas after her victories – and a bath house.

THE ROSE RED CITY

Almost impregnable in its remote valley among the Edom mountains in the south Jordanian desert, Petra is another city abandoned after a brief period of glory. Described by Strabo early in the 1st century AD as peaceful and well-governed, with caravans converging on it from the south or east, its great days as a trading city were already fading when Trajan annexed it in AD106, but it had once surpassed Palmyra. Debate continues about the exact date of its most famous monuments, the rockcut façades – some scholars date them before the Roman occupation, others after it – but their architecture is remarkably original. Situated in the Siq gorge between towering

mountain, Petra is built of the local reddish sandstone – hence its nickname "the Rose Red City". The visitor today first sees the Khasneh, or Treasury, with a remarkable central kiosk in the middle of its broken pediment. The same design is seen in Petra's most majestic building, the mausoleum called the Deir. Its façade is massive – 150ft long by 125ft high (46 by 38m) – larger than the west front of Westminster Abbey. However, it remains only a façade with a style that deserves the name baroque. Lost completely in its valley after its decline, Petra was only rediscovered in the 19th century.

Above: Façade of the Khasneh or Treasury at Petra, which has a circular kiosk in the middle of its broken pediment, an architectural extravagance typical of a style sometimes called Roman baroque. It was never a treasury, but was later thought to contain treasure by tomb robbers.

NÎMES AND ARLES: CITIES OF ROMAN GAUL

Julius Caesar called Gallia Transalpina *nostra provincia* (our province), because southern Gaul (today Languedoc and Provence) had been Roman since 121BC, and had long been influenced by Greek colonies such as Marseilles and Nice. Narbonne, which gave the province its later name Gallia Narbonensis, was Rome's first colony outside Italy, founded in 118BC. Under Augustus, the province thrived, becoming almost a second Italy and so peaceful it could be governed by a senator without an army. Meanwhile Roman civilization spread up the Rhône valley into central Gaul, transforming the region, with Lyons (Lugdunum) as its central city. Lyons' theatre, odeum, aqueducts and amphitheatre are all well-preserved.

Nîmes (Nemausus) was founded as a legionary veterans' colony in 35BC on the site of an earlier tribal capital and shrine to Nemausus, Gallic god of the local spring. In 16BC Augustus endowed his

new city with walls nearly four miles (6.4km) long, enclosing an area of about 500 acres (200ha). These walls, by then as much status symbol as military requirement, were 8ft wide (2.5m) and had 19 towers, of which the highest is the Tour Magne, a 130ft (40m) octagonal tower. A fine gateway has survived with two arches for wheeled traffic and two smaller side arches for pedestrians.

CLASSICISM IN THE PROVINCES

One of the best-preserved and most elegant of all Roman temples is the Maison Carrée (literally square house), which was begun in 19BC and dedicated to Augustus and his *gens* (family) – the imperial cult flourished outside Italy even while Augustus was still alive. Influenced by contemporary buildings in Rome, especially the Temple of Mars Ultor and the Ara Pacis (Altar of Peace), this is a superb example of Augustan classicism transplanted to the provinces, indeed possibly even built by the same craftsmen, with mathematically perfect proportions: its podium, columns and entablature are related in the ratio of 2:5:2. Nîmes' amphitheatre, dating from the late 1st century AD, has survived well. Its creators were clearly inspired by the Colosseum (Flavian Amphitheatre) built shortly before in Rome, as well as by the older Theatre of Marcellus, for they used the now standard motifs: arches framed by pilasters on the ground tier and by engaged columns in the second.

The Romans had realized very early on that Nîmes' spring waters would be inadequate for the growing colony. An aqueduct built by Agrippa or in the later 1st century AD brought water from near Uzès 31 miles (50km) away. Mostly this flowed in a channel buried underground or carried on a low wall, at a gentle 1:3,000 slope, but where the line crosses

Above: The Tour Magne, Nîmes, an octagonal tower 130ft (40m) high above the walls built by Augustus.

Below: Perhaps the most striking section of all aqueducts, the Pont du Gard crosses the gorge of the Gardon River.

Right: The calm elegance of the Maison Carrée at Nîmes shows how successfully Augustan classical ideals were transplanted to southern Gaul.

the gorge of the river Gardon, the most celebrated Roman aqueduct bridge was constructed: the Pont du Gard. Built entirely of squared stone, without clamps or mortar but with some individual stones weighing six tons, it is 295yds (269m) long and carries the water over the valley at a height of 160ft (49m) above the stream. Its proportions are simple yet aesthetically satisfying: four units for the central arch, three for the lateral arches, one for the upper tier of arches and six for the height of the whole structure. Its many projecting bosses were left to support scaffolding when repairs were needed. Inside the city the water flowed into large circular settling tanks from which outlets carried the water through-out the city. At its peak *c.* AD100, Nîmes had a population of possibly 50,000, so a copious water supply was needed.

THE LAST CAPITAL OF ROMAN GAUL
On the banks of the Rhône, which became an important trade route, Arles (Arelate) rivalled Nîmes as a wealthy, increasingly sophisticated city under the Principate (30BC–AD285), but it was also important in the empire's last days. The first legionary colony was founded in 46BC by Caesar after his Gallic conquests. Arles' two outstanding earlier Roman monuments still extant are its amphitheatre and its theatre. The amphitheatre is probably contemporary with that of its rival in Nîmes (AD80–100). The same architect, Crispius Reburrus, is thought to have designed both in the same essentially classic style. The theatre nearby resembles that of Aosta just across the Alps in northern Italy, in that the outer extremes of its *scaenae frons* (stage backdrop) was straight, not curved and its central door stands in a porch at the back of a shallow curved *exedra*, suggesting transalpine links.

The vaulted remains of a double portico lie beneath what must have been the Forum. Arles' town walls, again initially more ornamental than functional, resembled those of some Italian cities. They were strengthened in the 4th century AD when Arles was becoming increasingly important. The site of the first imperially sanctioned Church Council in AD314, Arles became the military headquarters of the westernmost empire after Trier was abandoned in AD395. It was briefly the capital of the pretender Constantine from Britain in AD407–9. Much grander imperial-style baths survive from this period. Arles was one of the last Gallic cities to remain in Roman control as the Western empire finally disintegrated in the AD450s.

Below: Remains of seating substructure at the amphitheatre at Arles dating from the late 1st century AD.

ROMANO-BRITISH CITIES

Above: Unearthed in Southwark in 2002, this plaque is inscribed with the name Londinium and dedicated to the god Mars. It is the oldest evidence of London's Roman name.

Below: This vivid mosaic of a horse is typical of the colourful decorations of the Roman baths at Bath.

Pre-Roman Britain had no cities in the Graeco-Roman sense and few cities apparently survived the Roman withdrawal of *c.* AD407. However, most Roman cities – London, York, Bath, Leicester, Chester, Winchester – later revived to show that the Romans had chosen their sites with typical acumen. Colchester, rather than London, was the Romans' first urban settlement and also their first British colony.

Two very different places, London, the great commercial centre that became the province's capital and Bath, the pleasure town, exemplify the Romano-British city.

LONDON
At the lowest possible crossing point on the Thames, Londinium was the merchants' preferred site and an important port, whether or not there was a Celtic settlement there earlier (the name Lun is Celtic). During Boudicca's revolt in AD60, the Britons killed a reported 70,000 Romanized traders in London and St Albans so it must have already been very populous. Tacitus said that London was "Crowded with traders, a hive of commerce". By *c.* 100AD it had acquired a governor's palace, a military fort on the north-east of the city covering 11 acres (4.45 h), a bridge across the Thames – initially in wood, later rebuilt in stone – and the city had probably become the administrative capital.

London retained its role as capital of Britannia Superior after the province was subdivided *c.* AD200. When Constantius I recovered Britain for the empire in AD296 from the rebel Allectus, London's citizens were so overjoyed by Constantius' troops' timely arrival to rescue them from Allectus' pillaging Frankish mercenaries that they hailed him as "Restorer of the eternal light". In the 4th century AD London received the title *Augusta*, indicating continued high status. Written records are few, however, and subsequent rebuilding has destroyed most of the archaeological remains.

One building was exceptional: London's basilica, beneath modern Gracechurch Street. The largest in the empire north of the Alps, comparable to a cathedral in scale and grandeur, it must have overwhelmed the north side of London's forum. A modest basilica had been erected under Domitian (ruled AD81–96) but when Hadrian visited Britain in AD122 – and ordered his wall built across northern England – it was massively reconstructed. (A coin of his reign has been found in its mortar.) The new building's main hall was around 49ft (192m) long, 115ft wide (35m) and about 89ft (27m) high. With triple aisles, it probably had apses at either end and statues such as the famous bronze bust of the emperor found in the Thames, but none have survived *in situ*. Refurbished in the 3rd century, it was demolished for unknown reasons in the 4th century AD.

Right: The Roman baths at Bath, where hot water bubbles out of the earth. Although other areas of the baths are still roofed, this section is now open to the sky.

One of the few Roman buildings now in the open is the temple to Mithras near the Mansion House. Built *c.* 200AD, it was about 60ft (19m) long, divided into a nave and two aisles by a row of columns, with an apse at one end. Later, other cult images, including Minerva, Serapis and Dionysus were added. These are among the finest found in Britain and make the temple almost a pantheon.

London's walls probably date from the reign of Caracalla (AD211–17) because a coin of his reign has been found in one section. They enclose an area of about 330 acres (132ha). Today, with few changes, these walls, which are about 3 miles (4.8km) long, mark the line and base of the medieval city walls and the boundaries of the City of London, although the street plan has changed. In the 330s AD, a wall reusing masonry and bits of sculpture was built along the Thames for the first time. After Count Theodosius' restoration of authority in Britain in AD367, London's walls were strengthened with projecting polygonal bastions incorporating not just old building materials but even tombs. By then, the city's population must have fallen from its 2nd-century peak of 35–40,000 people.

A ROMAN SPA TOWN

The Celts had worshipped the goddess Sulis at the place where hot waters bubble out of the ground at 125°F (46.5°C). The Romans, identifying her with their Minerva, developed Aquae Sulis ("the waters of Sulis", Bath) as a religious sanctuary and fashionable spa. The spring was given a stone pool to create a head of water. This supplied what became a remarkable bath complex, part of which has recently been restored. At its centre was the Great Bath, a lead-lined swimming-pool with a wooden roof, later under a vault, with other smaller baths with

heated water to the west. North of the spring a temple to Sulis/Minerva was built in a colonnaded courtyard. It had four Composite-style columns on a base about 29ft (9m) wide. The gap between the columns was twice their diameter of 2.6ft (0.8m), an unusual ratio that was also found in the Temple of Fortuna Virilis in Rome. The columns supported an entablature containing a relief of a Medusa-like male head in a shield carried by flanking winged Victories. There is a Celtic air to these carvings, in contrast to the distinctly Roman temple itself.

The baths were obviously successful and the complex continued to be extended into the 4th century AD, when the temple may have acquired flanking chapels. All the Roman ruins now lie about 20ft (6m) below street level.

Below: Bust of Hadrian, in whose reign (AD117–38) London gained an immense new basilica.

INDEX

Above: The Forum Romanum.

Above: Coin of Nero

Above: The Thermal Baths.

Left: A reconstruction drawing showing the Circus Maximus.